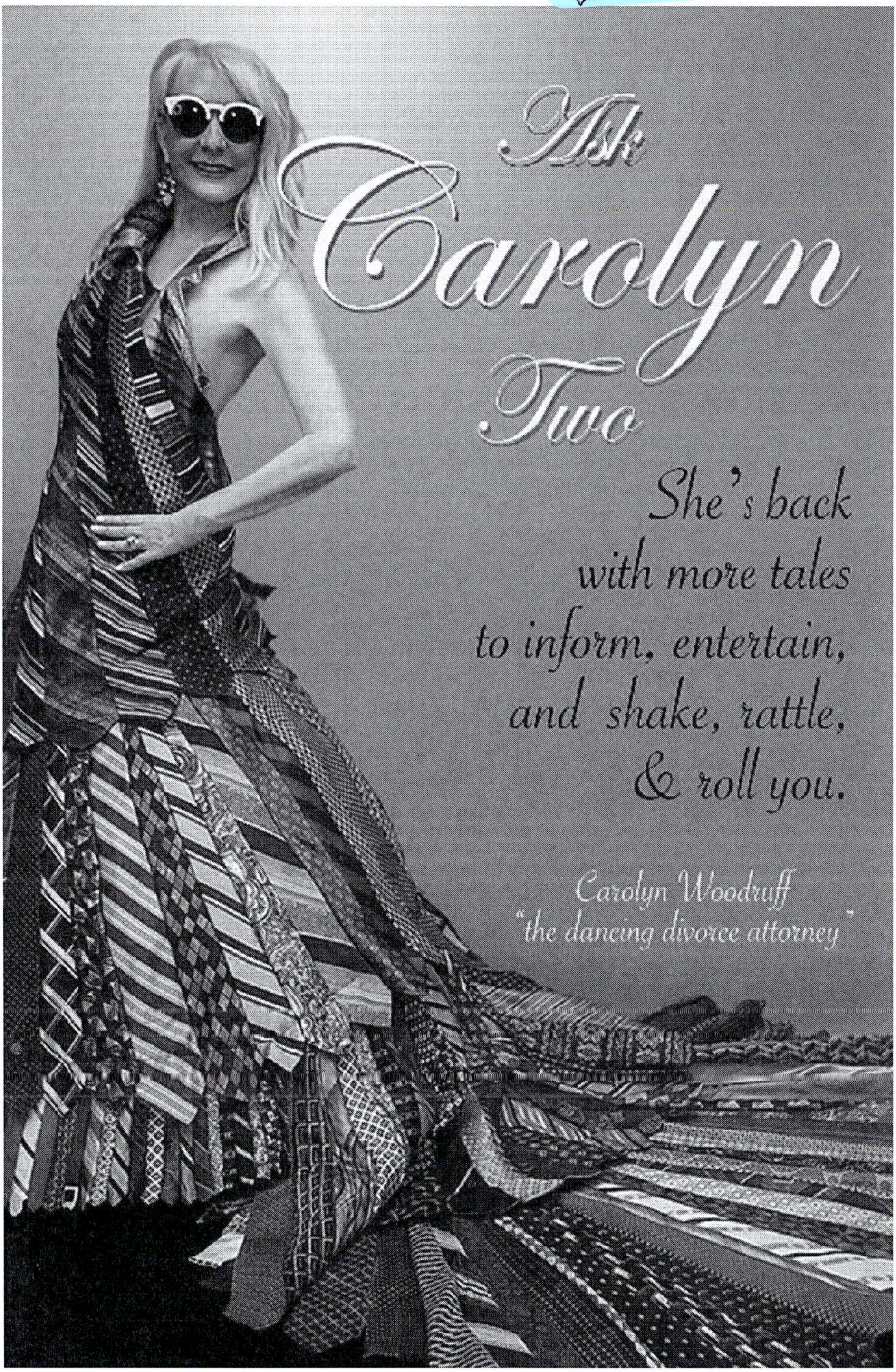
Ask
Carolyn
Two
She's back
with more tales
to inform, entertain,
and shake, rattle,
& roll you.
Carolyn Woodruff
"the dancing divorce attorney"

Woodruff Family Law Group

Copyright © 2016 Carolyn J. Woodruff

PUBLISHER:
Cupcake Buddies, LLC
420 West Market Street
Greensboro, NC 27401

ISBN: 978-1-940010-02-1

All rights reserved. No part of this book may be reproduced or transmitted in any form by any means, electronic or mechanical, including photocopying, recording, or by any information storage and retrieval system, without permission in writing from the publisher.

Everlasting thanks to my precious, loving husband, Dwight A. Ensley.

A special thanks to the following:
Roy Carroll, Publisher of **Rhino Times**
John Hammer, Editor-in-Chief of **Rhino Times**
Elaine Hammer, Managing Editor of **Rhino Times**

Without these fine folks, this book would not have happened.

For more questions and answers like you find in this book, please see the biweekly column in the *Rhino Times* named "Ask Carolyn ... Straight Talk from the Dancing Divorce Attorney." You can also find archived columns on *www.rhinotimes.com* and click on "columns."

ALSO, Carolyn is a blogger.
See *www.northcarolinadivorcelawyersblog.com*

# DEDICATED TO

*Martha Hereford Johnson, My Paternal Grandmother*
*(1894–1971)*

### The Cameo

I have a keepsake treasure of my grandmother's cameo brooch. The cameo is an intricate carving surrounded by gold. My grandmother's cameo is a carving of a strong, chiseled woman. She wore it often, and it was her signature piece. What a woman she was. She, along with my father (her son) are the two most influential people in my life. My father was Thomas Johnson, who died in 2002.

She grew up in Alabama, in a family of 10—six boys and four girls. The world was far different when she was born. Women didn't even have the right to vote, which is something that is very hard for me to imagine. My father was born in 1916, and women got the right to vote with the 19th Amendment to the U.S. Constitution, which was ratified August 18, 1920. So that sets the stage.

She was a woman who did not accept obstacles. When my father graduated high school, she moved with my dad and Morgan Johnson (Dad's older brother), to Tuscaloosa so my dad and his brother could attend the University of Alabama. She earned an entrepreneurial income by running a college boarding house for young men so my dad could get his B.A. degree in business administration, which he accomplished in 1937.

She was an entrepreneur ahead of her time. Her work ethic was incredible. She and her sister Lucy started the first convenience store in Tuscaloosa on a corner that still has a convenience store today. She owned and ran the store, making deals with farmers for eggs and produce and providing a novel, yet convenient store for her neighborhood.

She was a Renaissance woman with many talents, including creative talents. I still have some of her tatting, a very intricate lace she made. She taught me swimming and to ride a bike. We gardened and planted beautiful flowers. She was staunchly Christian, and I remember staying with her and seeing her up the wee hours of the morning reading her Bible. She was an active Presbyterian and community leader.

She gave me affirmations that women were equal to men, without actually discussing the issue. Looking back on the topic of women's equality, I never questioned that women were equal, even though in hindsight, that issue was right under my nose with a biological mother with no self-esteem who believed that boy children were superior to girl children. My grandmother, along with my father, rescued me. It is only after the passing of both my grandmother and my father that I realize how at risk I could have been. They shielded me from the insidious sexism of my biological mother, who clearly favored my brother at every turn. My grandmother encouraged me to strive to be all I could be and let nothing get in the way.

She died suddenly of a massive heart attack in 1971. I had just stayed at her house for a month that summer, but I never got to say good-bye. She wanted to see me graduate from high school, a goal beyond her control to achieve. She missed my valedictory address, but in that speech, I dared everyone to achieve and let *nothing* get in the way.

Yes, that cameo brooch of a strong, carved woman symbolized my grandmother. I am proud to be the granddaughter of Martha Hereford Johnson, and to her, I dedicate this book.

## DISCLAIMER

The questions and answers in this book are intended to provide general legal information for **North Carolina** cases. The answers are NOT specific legal advice for your specific situation. Your specific legal problem may have facts or even nuances not addressed in a particular answer. Please understand that you are not creating an attorney-client relationship with Carolyn J. Woodruff and/or Woodruff Family Law Group, 420 West Market Street, Greensboro, NC 27401, by purchasing or reading this book. For more legal information on family law topics, see *www.woodrufflawfirm.com*.

# About the Author

Carolyn J. Woodruff is a North Carolina Board Certified Family Law Specialist with more than 20 years' experience in family law. She is the founder and managing attorney of Woodruff Family Law Group at 420 West Market Street, Greensboro, NC 27401. She is a North Carolina Certified Public Accountant and a Certified Valuation Analyst of businesses. She is a graduate of Duke Law School with high honors, and she was Research and Managing Editor of the *Duke Law Journal*.

While Carolyn handles a full caseload at Woodruff Family Law Group, she spends much of her time giving back to the community by sharing her passion for ballroom dance. Ballroom dance was Carolyn's personal divorce recovery program. At age 40, she had never danced, but a former friend suggested that she try five things she had never tried before but had always wanted to try. So here's the bucket list: dance, flying, billiards, motorcycles, and scuba diving. Out of these, dance and flying became life-changing. Carolyn, along with Alosha Anatoliy of Fred Astaire Greensboro, have become three-time Fred Astaire Ballroom Dance National Smooth Champions and Fred Astaire Cabaret Champions. Carolyn and Alosha are Gold Best of the Best Show Dance Champions and have made five appearances in the New York Show, *Dance Legends*. She and Alosha also appeared in Moscow, in *Star Duo*, televised with 80 million viewers on Russia 2. In addition, Carolyn does showdance in the community, with her husband, Dwight.

Carolyn and her husband, Dwight Ensley, are coauthors of the children's holiday book, *The Seven Nights of Santa*. Captain Green Eyes, a black cat that flies a biplane, is the hero of the book. The book is for small children, their parents, grandparents, and caregivers. As an inspiration from the book, Carolyn started the Captain Green Eyes Dance Troupe, with the Boys and Girls Club in Greensboro, a free summer dance camp for children.

Carolyn also is a private pilot and enjoys flying a single-engine Piper Cherokee Archer, 180.

OTHER BOOKS BY CAROLYN WOODRUFF

*Ask Carolyn ... Straight Talk from the Dancing Divorce Attorney*

*Seven Nights of Santa,*
Coauthored with Dwight A. Ensley

# Prologue

*Ask Carolyn Two* changes format from *Ask Carolyn … Straight Talk from the Dancing Divorce Attorney*. This *Ask Carolyn Two* includes blogs published by Carolyn, as well as new columns she has written for the *Rhino Times*.

Carolyn writes from her experience as a family and divorce lawyer in North Carolina for many years. In this book, she also writes from her experience as a tax attorney and CPA on the difficult topics of Innocent Spouse Relief and Alimony Taxation. She also reveals topics close to her heart in Divorce Recovery. Technology and Social Media join this book as well. She discusses Critical Issues for Same-Sex Marriage in her final chapter.

Enjoy, and Ask Carolyn!

# Table of Contents

**CHAPTER 1**

Alimony and Post-Separation Support ............................................. 1
    General Overview ........................................................................ 1
    Entitlement: Who, How Much, and How Long? ..................... 2
    Substance Abuse as a Determining Factor ................................ 4
    When Are Payments Tax Deductible? ....................................... 6

**CHAPTER 2**

Innocent Spouse Relief ..................................................................... 7
    General Overview ........................................................................ 7
    Proving Tax Fraud ....................................................................... 8
    Innocent Husband Wins in Tax Court ...................................... 9
    Separation and Divorce—Important Factors .......................... 11
    Recipe for Innocent Spouse Relief ........................................... 12
    Third-Party Evidence and Credibility Are Key ....................... 14

**CHAPTER 3**

Alimony Taxation ............................................................................ 16
    General Overview ...................................................................... 16
    Tax Dangers of Unallocated Family Support .......................... 16
    An Alimony Deduction Fatality ............................................... 18
    "Death Termination" for Alimony Deduction ........................ 20

## CHAPTER 4

Premarital Agreements .................................................................... 22
   General Overview ...................................................................... 22
   Should I Get a Premarital Agreement? ................................... 23
   Planning for Your Future "Former" Spouse .......................... 24
   Parents, Children, and Premarital Agreements .................... 25
   Gray Marriage—Plan Wisely! .................................................. 27
   Procedures for Signing ............................................................. 29
   My Fiancé Wants a Prenupt—I Don't Want to Sign! .......... 31

## CHAPTER 5

Divorce ................................................................................................ 33
   General Overview ...................................................................... 33
   Grounds for Divorce ................................................................. 33
   Divorce of Bed and Board: Sneak Attack! ............................. 36
   Do-It-Yourself-Divorce Advice ................................................ 37
   Basic Divorce Procedure in NC ............................................... 39
   Protecting Your Credit .............................................................. 40

## CHAPTER 6

Divorce Recovery .............................................................................. 42
   General Overview ...................................................................... 42
   Back in the Saddle ..................................................................... 43
   Second-Marriage Considerations ............................................ 44
   Surviving the Holidays ............................................................. 46
   Divorce Recovery Tip ............................................................... 47

## CHAPTER 7

Domestic Violence ............................................................................ 48
   General Overview ...................................................................... 48
   Facebook Threats ....................................................................... 50
   Cyberstalking ............................................................................. 51
   Confronting Sexual Abuse ....................................................... 53
   Expiring Protective Order ........................................................ 54

Gun Possession in Domestic Violence Cases ........................................ 56
Presenting Drug Paraphernalia as Evidence ........................................ 58

## CHAPTER 8

Property Division ................................................................................ 60
    General Overview ........................................................................... 60
    Protecting Business during Separation ........................................... 61
    Ex-Spouse Hiding Assets ................................................................ 62
    Estate Planning and In-Laws .......................................................... 63
    Qualified Domestic Relations Order ............................................. 65
    College Funds in Equitable Distribution ....................................... 65

## CHAPTER 9

Technology and Social Media ............................................................. 68
    General Overview ........................................................................... 68
    FaceTime Visitation ........................................................................ 68
    GPS Tracking .................................................................................. 70
    Spyware ........................................................................................... 71
    Caught by the iPad! ........................................................................ 73

## CHAPTER 10

Miscellaneous ....................................................................................... 75
    Collaborative Law .......................................................................... 75
    Critical Issues for Same-Sex Marriage ........................................... 77
    Un-Neighborly Conduct ................................................................ 79
    Ungrateful Relatives ....................................................................... 80
    Adult Children and Substance Abuse ........................................... 81

# CHAPTER 1

# Alimony and Post-Separation Support

## ▞ GENERAL OVERVIEW

In North Carolina, you may be entitled to alimony if you are the **dependent spouse**. This means you are actually substantially dependent upon the other spouse for support or substantially in need of support from the other spouse.

It must be **equitable** to award the dependent spouse alimony. Equitable is determined on the following relevant factors:

- Financial needs of the parties;
- Accustomed standard of living;
- Present employment income and other recurring earnings of each party from any source;
- Earning abilities of both spouses;
- Separate and marital debt service obligations;
- Living expenses of both parties necessary for support of each;
- Each party's respective legal obligations to support any other person.

Finally, illicit sexual behavior plays a determinative role in entitlement to permanent alimony.

*a.* If you are the dependent spouse, and you engaged in uncondoned illicit sexual behavior during the marriage and prior to the date of separation, you will not be entitled to alimony unless the supporting spouse also participated in an act of uncondoned illicit sexual behavior during the marriage prior to the date of separation.

*b.* If you are the supporting spouse, your spouse shall be entitled to alimony if you engaged in an uncondoned illicit sexual act during the marriage prior to the date of separation (and the dependent spouse is not guilty of the same conduct).

If both spouses have engaged in an uncondoned illicit sexual act, then alimony may be denied or awarded in the discretion of the court after consideration of all the other circumstances.

## ENTITLEMENT: WHO, HOW MUCH, AND HOW LONG?

Dear Carolyn:

I work and make a good income. During our marriage, my wife worked for a while but stopped when we had children. She has and maintains a CPA license. We have a 15-year-old with some discipline problems and ADHD. We are divorcing, and I think she should go back to work. She wants alimony. Who is right? Does she need to work, or can she just continue to be a leech?

*Anti-Leech*

Carolyn Answers ...

Dear Anti-Leech,

I certainly understand the frustration you are facing. I'll give you some tips for preparing your case, particularly regarding whether the court should impute income to your ex-wife. You will want to study carefully the case of *Nicks v. Nicks* from the North Carolina Court of Appeals in June 2015, which discusses the topic of imputation of income.

You have an excellent case that your wife should apply for and obtain employment as a CPA. The only issue you raise is whether your child's situation justifies your wife staying home. The North Carolina Child Support Guidelines by analogy indicate that the judge cannot impute to a parent staying home with a child under 3.

In *Nicks*, the couple was married 26 years and had four children, with only one still a minor. The child was in the tenth grade, and the mother expressed concern for the child's mental well-being. The wife was a physician, and she had recently worked, but the clinic closed. Before the clinic closed, the wife was making $8,000 per month. The trial court imputed $8,000 per month income to the wife, and the wife appealed to the North Carolina Court of Appeals. The husband had $19,000 of disability income per month as a disabled physician, which ended at his age 65. The wife needed around $11,000 per month for her needs, according to the trial court. The Court of Appeals remanded (sent back) the case to the trial court to determine if the physician wife was suppressing her income in "bad faith" as defined by the *Works* decision from 2011.

In *Works*, the Court of Appeals indicated the income could be imputed if a party has depressed her/his income in "bad faith." "Bad faith" is defined as "shirking the duty of self-support." A spouse refusal to seek or to accept gainful employment is "bad faith."

After consideration of *Works*, the Court of Appeals in *Nicks* remanded (sent back for further findings) to the trial court regarding whether the wife in *Nicks* was acting in "bad faith."

Good luck with getting your ex-wife back to work as a CPA.

Dear Carolyn:

My wife had an affair, and because I wanted to save the marriage for the children, I forgave her. That was about 10 years ago. Now, it is really not working, and I want out. The last child has finished high school. My wife spends too much money, and she will not find a job. She says I owe her alimony if I leave. She has the same college degree I do. Can she get alimony? What about her affair?

*I tried, but … just can't do it anymore …*

Carolyn Answers ...

Dear "I Tried,"

Theoretically, your wife may get alimony if you are the supporting spouse and she is the dependent spouse. However, there is some good news for you in this answer. First, I do want to explain the doctrine of condonation. Also, please note that I use "adultery," "affair," and "illicit sexual misconduct" interchangeably in this answer. The official language in the North Carolina alimony statutes is now "illicit sexual misconduct."

In family law, condonation means forgiveness. So you condoned the affair with your forgiveness; otherwise, an affair (illicit sexual misconduct) is a bar to alimony. "Bar" means absolute barrier. So, unless you were also guilty of an affair, you would not have paid her alimony if you had left when she had the affair 10 years ago. But, the forgiveness now makes you vulnerable for paying alimony. Now for the good news!

In the recent Charlotte case of *Ellis v. Ellis*, the trial judge considered the wife's past adultery (although forgiven by the husband) as a factor in setting the amount and duration of alimony. The North Carolina Court of Appeals affirmed (agreed with) the Charlotte judge, so now we have guidance on how to use forgiven adultery in cases.

In *Ellis*, the wife called herself a "bored housewife" as justification for the affair and had an affair with a professional hockey player. This "bored housewife" certainly should not have used these words with the judge. When testifying, select your words carefully. The Charlotte judge only gave her 2 years of alimony, enough for letting her find a suitable job, but not long enough to reward her for her misconduct. Hopefully, this will cure her boredom.

You are also going to be able to use that fact, that your wife is a spendthrift, against her. Tell her "Ask Carolyn," says: Get a job!

## SUBSTANCE ABUSE AS A DETERMINING FACTOR

Dear Carolyn:

I think my spouse has alcohol addiction, and I do not know what to do. He is ruining our lives, but he is still able to work. I confronted him about the alcohol, and he has started hiding it. I found vodka hidden in the spare bathroom in a place I do not ordinarily look. I don't work, and I haven't worked for more than 10 years. We have a comfortable lifestyle. What should I do to help him? Will I get alimony if I leave? He can afford to pay me at least something, and I will get a job.

*Undecided*

Carolyn Answers ...

Dear Undecided,

I'll answer both of your questions although treatises could be written on these issues. Please take this information as a general place of starting to understand the alcohol addiction problem and its effect on marriage. First, I'll address some dos and don'ts of dealing with an alcoholic spouse. Second, I'll address alcohol as a fault factor regarding alimony in North Carolina.

I think the three basic things to do (as a start) are as follows:

1. You should speak up. Offer your support and try to find help without being judgmental. Be prepared for denial.
2. You should be safe yourself. You cannot get caught up in the problem, and you need someone to talk to about this. You might try Al-Anon.
3. You should avoid self-blame. This is not your fault.

Here are some don'ts:

1. Don't retaliate or punish.
2. Don't use emotional appeals as this may increase guilt feelings and increase the compulsion for alcohol.
3. Don't cover for the alcohol user or shield him from the negative consequences of the behavior.
4. Don't argue with the person when he is drunk.
5. Don't feel guilty yourself.

Now, I'll turn to alcohol as a factor in determining alimony. In North Carolina, excessive use of alcohol is a factor for the judge to consider in the duration and amount of alimony if this evidence is presented. You need to gather your evidence. Helpful evidence might be any of the following: (1) receipts for the purchase of booze; (2) photographs of bottles or even your spouse passed out on the couch; (3) DWI criminal records; (4) recordings of arguments while drunk; (5) video of incidents; (6) witness affidavits; and (7) any other proof you may have.

Keep your evidence in a safe place away from the marital residence.

## WHEN ARE PAYMENTS TAX DEDUCTIBLE?

Dear Carolyn:

I have been paying my estranged wife support of $2,500 per month since February 2014 when we separated. My CPA says I cannot deduct the $2,500 per month on my 2014 taxes. I simply do not understand. I'm a good guy, and she actually got the support. Why isn't this alimony?

*Tired of Paying*

Carolyn Answers ...

Dear Tired of Paying,

Oh boy, and I am sorry, but the Internal Revenue Code only recognizes money as deductible alimony that is paid pursuant to a valid North Carolina marital agreement for alimony or post-separation support or a court order. A valid North Carolina marital agreement done outside of court must have each former spouse's (estranged spouse's) signature notarized.

Do you have a family law attorney? If not, you need to get one immediately. I would recommend that you see a family law attorney and get the proper writing. Consider not making any more payments until you get the written agreement, as you are going to have the same problems with the 2015 payments of voluntary spousal support. Even letters between two attorneys regarding spousal support are not enough. Get an official agreement on this. Good luck!

# CHAPTER 2

# Innocent Spouse Relief

## ▚ GENERAL OVERVIEW

I deal almost every day with joint income tax returns that are incorrectly prepared and now the two, who filed the joint return, are divorcing. Who is responsible for the error with the Internal Revenue Service? A joint return is a joint and severe liability, meaning that both people are responsible for all of the taxes, and the IRS will get it first wherever it is easiest to collect.

In the 1990s, I was a member of the Domestic Relations Tax Committee, Tax Section, of the American Bar Association. As a leader on that committee, I sought reform and relief for the innocent spouse who was the person who did not prepare the return. The result of our effort is Section 6015 of the Internal Revenue Code that gives substantial possibility of relief to victims of tax return financial abuse, particularly those going through a divorce.

The chapter deals with some of the hot topics regarding innocent spouses. While the best option is to never file a joint tax return with a tax cheat, the next best option is to apply for innocent spouse relief. Innocent spouse cases are fact driven, and the history of the victim's abuse, both physical and financial, are important to the innocent spouse case.

## PROVING TAX FRAUD

Dear Carolyn:

I have an example of corruption that exists in the family court system in North Carolina. My ex-wife is requesting increased child support. When I requested all of her financial documents, she provided fraudulent tax returns to the courts in order to gain increased child support payments from me. When I advised the judge of the fraudulent tax returns and proof that I had as far as lease for rental property that she claimed zero income for 2 out of 3 years, the judge's comment was she is not the IRS, therefore, allowing felony fraud to be committed in her courtroom and participating in a conspiracy to commit felony fraud.

*Exposing Corruption*

Carolyn Answers ...

Dear Exposing Corruption,

Your saga is one of my favorite topics, so thank you for calling Sound of the Beep. It is unclear to me if you are in Guilford County, as we technically do not have a "family court system" in Guilford. Randolph County does have a family court. It also sounds like you are representing yourself.

When you are going to challenge someone's income tax return, you must provide convincing and complete evidence. For example, you might compel the attendance of the renter of the real estate to court and ask the renter to bring with him copies of rental payments to your ex. You do this with a document called a subpoena. You might provide photos of the rental property with the renter's car in the driveway, and the deed to the rental property. Perhaps, your ex deposited the rental payments into her checking account; thus, obtaining and presenting the checking account statements would help your situation. Obtaining via subpoena the electricity records and water bills from the providers for the 3 years in question would show that someone was in the rental house and probably would even provide the name of the renter. What you must have in a situation like this is lots of corroborating (or confirming) evidence.

INNOCENT SPOUSE RELIEF  9

If you simply went to court and said, "I know she has rental income" without some proof, the judge might rightly ignore you. But you also had the right to cross-examine your ex regarding her rental property, who the renter is, and how much the renter pays her per month. You had the right to call your ex to the witness stand and ask her about the rental income. Did you do this?

You also have a Rule 60 Motion you could file within 1 year of the court date you describe. The motion would allege the fraud. Rule 60 permits the judge to correct the injustice of the missing rental income. But, make doubly sure you have issued the subpoena you need to prove your case.

On another note, you might simply turn your ex into the IRS and try to get the 10 percent finder's fee. That might be fun!

Don't give up, and you probably need a family law attorney to help with the proof of income. Make sure the attorney is competent in income tax-proof issues.

Carolyn Blogs On ...

## INNOCENT HUSBAND WINS IN TAX COURT

In North Carolina, as well as nationwide, family law and divorce cases are filled with bad tax returns. Let's face it, generally one spouse handles the finances and the other spouse doesn't. Enjoy *Santa* as the tax court finds this husband innocent.

### Santa v. Comm'r, T.C. Memo. 2013-78, 2013 WL 3984636 (2013)

a. **Facts:** The wife suffered from various addictions and often hid financial matters from the husband. She obtained a credit card without the husband's knowledge and forged his name on a certificate of title on her vehicle so that she could sell it for cash. In 2002, she withdrew $95,392 from her retirement account without telling the husband. For portions of that year, the parties lived separately.

Please note that the parties were in a state of separation for some of 2002. The parties filed a joint tax return for 2002. The wife did not tell the preparer about the $95,392 withdrawal, or about some of her 2002 wage income. The IRS discovered the unreported income and assessed a deficiency.

The husband filed for innocent spouse relief. The IRS denied the request, and the husband appealed to the tax court. While the case was pending, he separated from the wife, and they eventually divorced. He did not notify the tax court of his change of address, the notice of trial was sent to the former marital home, and the husband never received it. As a result, he did not appear for trial, and the court denied his request for relief.

The IRS sent the parties a notice of tax lien to enforce the unpaid 2002 taxes. The husband filed a second request for innocent spouse relief. The IRS again denied the request, and the husband again appealed to the tax court.

b. **Issue:** Is the husband entitled to innocent spouse relief?

c. **Answer to Issue:** Yes.

d. **Summary of Rationale:** Under § 6015(c), innocent spouse relief is available if the parties are divorced or legally separated or physically separated for 12 months, and a tax understatement is attributable to the other spouse's income unless the IRS proves that the spouse requesting relief knew of the understatement.

The IRS argued that the prior decision denying innocent spouse relief was binding under principles of res judicata. But the parties had not yet been divorced or legally separated or physically separated for 12 months. Thus, Section 6015(c) relief was not available in the prior appeal, and the prior denial of relief was not res judicata.

The IRS claimed that the $95,392 was deposited into a joint bank account, but it presented no supporting evidence. The court accepted the husband's testimony that the money was placed into an account known only to the wife. Because the requirements of § 6015(c) were met, the husband was entitled to relief.

e. **Obvious Lesson:** When an appeal to the tax court is pending, notify the court of any change in address! Notice is especially important when your address of record is the former marital home with a spouse who has a very long history of dishonest behavior.

The husband was fortunate that § 6015(c) relief was not available in the first proceeding. If it had been available, the husband would have had a substantial res judicata problem.

Carolyn Blogs On ...

## SEPARATION AND DIVORCE—IMPORTANT FACTORS

*Molinet v. Comm'r*, T.C. Memo. 2014-109, 2014 WL 2573992 (2014)

a. **Facts:** A husband and wife were married. The wife was from Cuba and was admitted to the United States on a fiancée visa. The husband controlled the marital finances with minimal input from the wife. She had access to the parties' joint checking account, but rarely used it and did not have a good understanding of the United States banking system. She paid her expenses with a weekly allowance from the husband.

The parties initially lived in Maryland, but they moved to Florida for the wife's health. To finance the trip, the husband withdrew $117,191 from his 401(k) plan. The wife did not approve of the withdrawal but felt she had no choice and reluctantly signed documents regarding the withdrawal.

The parties' 2008 income tax return reported $30,938 in tax liability, much of it from the 401(k) plan withdrawal. The wife believed at the time that the husband could pay the amount due, as he had paid all other prior tax liabilities. Note that this retirement plan may have been a marital asset and possibly could have been "QDROed" (Qualified Domestic Relations Order) in the divorce.

The parties separated in 2008 and were divorced in 2009. The Florida divorce decree allocated the 2008 income tax debt to the husband.

The husband did not pay the 2008 tax debt, and the wife petitioned for discretionary innocent spouse relief under § 6015(f). The IRS denied relief, and the wife appealed to the tax court. The husband intervened, opposing relief. The IRS admitted at trial that the wife should receive relief, but the husband continued to argue otherwise.

b. **Issue:** Is the wife entitled to discretionary innocent spouse relief?

c. **Answer to Issue:** Yes.

   d. **Summary of Rationale:** The safe harbor rule does not apply, because the wife had not established that she would suffer economic hardship if forced to share liability for the taxes. Factors favoring relief included: (1) the parties were divorced, (2) the wife had little knowledge of marital finances and reasonably believed that the husband could pay the tax due; (3) the divorce decree allocated the tax debt entirely to the husband; (4) the funds withdrawn were used mostly to acquire a new home in Florida, which was awarded to the husband in the divorce case, so the wife did not benefit from nonpayment of taxes; (5) the wife had fully complied with tax law in all future tax years; and (6) the wife suffered from significant health problems. The court held that economic hardship was neutral, as the wife had a monthly income of $3,616 and monthly expenses of roughly $3,100. Because the balance of factors strongly supported relief, innocent spouse relief was granted.

   e. **Comments:**

      a. When the IRS favors innocent spouse relief, and the only party objecting is the intervening noninnocent spouse, the argument against innocent spouse relief is always especially hard to make.

      b. If innocent spouse relief had been denied, the wife could still have sued the husband under the divorce decree to be reimbursed for any portion of the debt she was forced to pay. The problem, however, is that the husband may not have had the funds to pay a state court judgment.

Carolyn Blogs On ...

## RECIPE FOR INNOCENT SPOUSE RELIEF

*Varela v. Comm'r*, T.C. Memo. 2014-222, 2014 WL 53656631 (2014)

   a. **Facts:** A husband and wife filed joint tax returns for 2007 and 2008. The IRS assessed deficiencies. The wife petitioned the tax court for innocent spouse relief, and the husband intervened, asking the court to deny the request. The court asked for briefs, and the husband failed to file one, but the court addressed the issues nevertheless.

The parties kept separate bank accounts during the years in question. The husband owned a business, JL Unique Homes, Inc. ("JL Unique"). The wife was initially a director but never did work for the company. She did, however, assist its office manager in organizing the company's paperwork.

The tax issue arose when the husband used certain business funds for personal purposes. The wife did not know of this use initially. The parties separated in 2009, and the wife did learn of the use during divorce proceedings.

b. **Issue:** Was the wife entitled to innocent spouse relief?

c. **Answer to Issue:** Yes.

d. **Summary of Rationale:** The IRS agreed that the wife was entitled to innocent spouse relief, so the only party objecting was the husband. The husband argued that the tax problem was partly attributable to the wife's conduct and that the wife should have known that the tax had not been paid.

The wife did not work for JL Unique and had no access to its bank accounts. "[E]ven though petitioner is listed as an incorporator and a director of JL Unique, she credibly testified that she never performed any services in that capacity. The company never issued formal stock certificates or other records that reflect its ownership, and petitioner never received a formal dividend from the company." 2014 WL 53656631, at *4. "We see no basis to conclude that petitioner was either formally or informally a shareholder of JL Unique, and, thus, the erroneous omission of constructive dividends from petitioner and intervenor's 2007 and 2008 joint returns was not the omission of items attributable to her." Id.

"Petitioner did not have access to either intervenor's or JL Unique's bank accounts and thus did not know that intervenor was withdrawing money from the company's accounts in 2007 and 2008 or that he was doing so without JL Unique's formally declaring a dividend." The wife knew that money was coming from JL Unique, "but nothing in the record indicates that she was aware that the funds were withdrawn inappropriately, or that intervenor failed to report them on their return." Id. at *5. Her lack of knowledge was especially justifiable because the husband "concealed the fact that the withdrawn funds were inappropriately taken from JL," *id.*, and because the wife received no benefit from the withdrawn funds beyond ordinary support. The wife is therefore entitled to innocent spouse relief.

e. ***Tactical Litigation Suggestion:*** If you are litigating in the tax court, and the court asks for briefs, it might be a good idea to file one.

Carolyn Blogs On ...

### THIRD-PARTY EVIDENCE AND CREDIBILITY ARE KEY

*Sapp v. Comm'r*, T.C. Memo. 2015-143, 2015 WL 4639260 (2015)

a. **Facts:** The IRS assessed deficiencies on a husband and wife's joint income tax returns for 2004, 2006, and 2008. The parties appealed to the tax court, and the wife sought both mandatory and discretionary innocent spouse relief. The IRS conceded that relief was appropriate, but the husband argued otherwise.

The tax at issue arose from the husband's plumbing business, for which the wife served as bookkeeper. There was a history of domestic abuse in the marriage going back to 2002. The parties had been separated multiple times, and the wife spent time living in a domestic violence shelter.

At the time of the tax court hearing, the parties were separated but not yet divorced. The wife had little income and was receiving food stamps.

b. **Issue:** Was the wife entitled to innocent spouse relief?

c. **Answer to Issue:** Yes.

d. **Summary of Rationale:** Because the wife served as bookkeeper for the business, she knew of the tax matters at issue, and she was not eligible for mandatory innocent spouse relief.

For discretionary innocent spouse relief, there is an exception to the knowledge requirement in cases of abuse. The court summarily held that abuse was present, so the threshold conditions were met.

Without addressing the "safe harbor" conditions, the court moved directly to the discretionary factors. Two factors were favorable: the parties were separated, and the wife would suffer financial hardship from paying the taxes. A third factor, the wife's knowledge of the tax problem, was superficially negative but is treated as favorable when abuse is present. Because all of the relevant factors were favorable, the court granted innocent spouse relief.

e. **Comments:** *Sapp* is another case that speaks directly to the reasons why the IRS is now considering abuse as a factor in innocent spouse cases.

   a. The court was rather demure in setting forth the details of the evidence. "Although we are reluctant to include details of the abuse to which Ms. Sapp testified, we find that there is a history of domestic abuse in their relationship dating back at least to the birth of their first son in 2002." 2015 WL 4639260, at *1. But abuse is a newly important factor in innocent spouse cases, and the requirements for proving abuse are an issue upon which hard law is needed. Some of the cases discussed in this outline suggest that the federal courts are seeing a wave of weak claims of abuse. An important tool in dealing with this wave is factual specificity in cases finding abuse so that the practicing bar will know what a strong case of abuse looks like. The court's reluctance to provide factual details does not help the federal courts work through the necessary process of defining abuse.

   b. The fact that the wife spent time in a domestic violence shelter was a solid piece of third-party evidence in favor of abuse.

   c. One suspects, however, that the primary factor driving the tax court's conclusion was simply its belief that the wife was credible. The only real piece of third-party evidence referred to is the wife's time in the domestic violence shelter. *Sapp* is, therefore, some evidence that a claim of abuse can be based primarily upon the abused spouse's testimony—*if* the tax court finds that testimony is credible.

# CHAPTER 3

# Alimony Taxation

## ▓ GENERAL OVERVIEW

In planning for your divorce, one of the areas for creativity in financial planning is alimony because of its tax deductibility to the payor. One can frequently arbitrage dollars for a payor with a higher tax rate and a payee with a lower tax rate, saving dollars that would otherwise go to the IRS.

As a family law specialist and North Carolina CPA, I have taught classes on alimony taxation for over 20 years now. To utilize the tool of alimony planning, one must have very specific knowledge of the elements of Section 71 of the Internal Revenue Code. This chapter deals with pitfalls that landed folks in the U.S. Tax Court on alimony and family support issues.

Carolyn Blogs On ...

## ▓ TAX DANGERS OF UNALLOCATED FAMILY SUPPORT

It is tempting to lump child support and post-separation support/alimony into a bucket of $1 amount, sometimes referred to as "family support." This is particularly tempting in the early part of a case, but it is DANGEROUS. A couple of tax rules will help:

- Rule 1: Don't create family support as a way to get 100 percent of support as an alimony deduction as this really doesn't work.

- Rule 2: Don't think you can sort out the tax consequence later. The IRS is suspicious, and there is substantial federal tax case law indicating that *nunc pro tunc* state court orders cannot alter tax consequences. You have to do it right the first time.

Note that North Carolina family law statutes do not have in them the concept of family support. North Carolina has three types of support: 1) child support; 2) alimony; 3) post-separation support. CPAs in North Carolina need to be particularly alert to mislabeling as "family support."

See how Mr. Baur lost most of his "alimony" deduction by violating Rules 1 and 2 above.

### *Baur v. Comm'r*, T.C. Memo. 2014-117, 2014 WL 2619658 (2014)

a. **Facts:** A divorce settlement agreement, incorporated into an Illinois divorce decree, required the husband to pay to the wife $3,750 per month in unallocated alimony and child support, plus 45 percent of any net bonuses received from his employer. The payments terminated upon the wife's remarriage or cohabitation, or upon the death of either party. If the children were emancipated and living without assistance from the wife, the payments dropped to $1,800 per month. The agreements were to constitute alimony for federal tax purposes.

   The husband paid support under the agreement and claimed an alimony deduction on his federal income tax return. The IRS disallowed a portion of the alimony deduction and assessed a deficiency. The husband appealed to the tax court.

   After the IRS had assessed a deficiency, the Illinois state court issued a nunc pro tunc order stating that all payments made under the agreement were intended as maintenance and not as child support. The order further provided that the provision reducing the payments upon the emancipation of the children was the result of a scrivener's error, and was stricken from the order.

b. **Issue:** Was the husband entitled to a full 100 percent alimony deduction for all of the payments made?

c. **Answer to Issue:** No.

d. **Summary of Rationale:** The payments were not expressly fixed as child support and stopped upon death. But payments are implicitly fixed as child support if they are reduced upon a child-related event. The emancipation provision clearly involved a child-related event, so the key issue was the effect of the nunc pro tunc state court order.

   The court rejected the state court order and held that the inclusion of the emancipation provision was not the result of a scrivener's error. Therefore, the husband was not entitled to an alimony deduction for the amount of the reduction.

e. **Comment:** The IRS was not a party to the state court proceedings, so it was not bound by the state court order, finding a scrivener's error. Attempts to fix tax problems with after-the-fact state court orders are likely to be viewed with suspicion by the IRS.

## Carolyn Blogs On ...

### AN ALIMONY DEDUCTION FATALITY

*Faylor* is an example of a good guy finishing last. It is an absolute requirement for an alimony deduction that the payment be made pursuant to a qualifying court decree for alimony or a qualifying private agreement for alimony. One signed after the fact does not give you a deduction for payments already made.

*Faylor* situations happen routinely in North Carolina, so it is important for the North Carolina family lawyer or the CPA to be diligent and avoid failing like *Faylor*. See what happened as there is no way to fix this alimony deduction problem after the fact.

*Faylor v. Comm'r*, T.C. Memo. 2013-143, 2013 WL 2435072 (2013)

a. **Facts:** A divorce case was filed in Nebraska. The wife's attorney sent the husband's attorney a letter demanding $6,000 per month in temporary alimony. The husband's attorney responded with an offer of $4,000 per month. The wife's attorney responded that the wife would accept $5,000 per month, and suggested that the husband's attorney draft an order. The attorneys then entered into a prolonged series of discussions over which party would be responsible for various expenses.
   No temporary support order was ever drafted or signed.

Nevertheless, starting soon after the wife's attorney stated that the wife would accept $5,000 per month, the husband began depositing $5,000 per month into a joint account to which the wife had access. He made these payments, intending that the wife use the payments for her support.

A divorce decree was eventually entered, requiring the husband to pay $2,500 per month in alimony. The husband claimed an alimony deduction for the $5,000-per-month payments he made before the decree was entered. The IRS disallowed the deduction and assessed a deficiency. The husband appealed to the tax court.

b. **Issue:** Was the husband entitled to an alimony deduction for payments made before entry of the final divorce decree?

c. **Answer:** No.

d. **Summary of Rationale:** The first requirement in the federal definition of alimony requires that the payment be made pursuant to a "divorce or separation instrument." I.R.C. § 71(b)(1)(A). A "divorce or separation instrument" means a divorce decree or a *written* separate agreement. *Id.* § 71(b)(2). The IRS argued that the $5,000 payments were not required by any decree or written agreement. The husband argued that the exchange of letters between counsels constituted a binding written agreement, requiring him to make the payments.

The court disagreed. "Letters which do not show a meeting of the minds between the parties cannot collectively constitute a written separation agreement." *Faylor*, 2013 WL 2435072, at *3. The letter showed disagreement on material terms involving payment of expenses, and indeed, both parties' divorce attorneys testified in tax court that no settlement had been reached. Because there was no meeting of minds, there was no written agreement, and the payments were not made pursuant to a "divorce or separation instrument." The husband was, therefore, not entitled to an alimony deduction.

e. **Lesson:** Do not take an alimony deduction unless a divorce decree or clear written agreement exists, requiring the taxpayer to make support payments to a spouse or former spouse. Informal or voluntary support is unlikely to constitute alimony for federal tax purposes.

Carolyn Blogs On ...

## "DEATH TERMINATION" FOR ALIMONY DEDUCTION

North Carolina alimony statutes and state case law make technicalities on the "death" element of alimony under federal tax law difficult, and one needs to exercise extreme care when drafting a private alimony agreement or contract in North Carolina.

Unlike many states, all alimony awards in North Carolina are not court orders. For legitimate strategic reasons, alimony awards are frequently private contracts in North Carolina. Generally, one cannot modify a contractual award of alimony, but court orders for alimony may be modifiable upon a change in circumstances. That scares many payors in North Carolina, so they negotiate for a private contract.

The trick is that North Carolina's alimony statutes provide that court-ordered alimony terminates upon the death of the recipient spouse, a requirement for deductibility of alimony under Section 71 of the Internal Revenue Code. The problem is that the North Carolina alimony statutes do not necessarily apply to private contracts for alimony, so one should specify that the alimony should terminate on the death of the payee spouse. Let's see what happened in *Wignall*. Note that *Wignall* is a court decree, not a private contract.

I.R.C. § 71(b)(1), (c)(1)-(2).

*Wignall v. Comm'r*, T.C. Memo. 2014-22, 2014 WL 303375 (2014)

a. **Facts:** An Oregon divorce decree required the husband to pay the wife $1,900 per month from July 2006 through December 2011. The decree did not expressly state whether the payments stopped upon the wife's death.

The husband paid the alimony and claimed a deduction. The IRS disallowed the deduction, and the husband appealed to the tax court.

b. **Issue:** Was the husband entitled to an alimony deduction?

c. **Answer to Issue:** Yes.

d. **Summary of Rationale:** The key issue was whether the obligation to pay alimony stopped upon the wife's death. Since the decree was silent, the court looked to Oregon state law.

"The right to receive alimony and the corresponding duty to pay it are generally considered to have terminated on the death of either of the two parties, at least where no statute to the contrary exists, and the judgment or decree is silent on the subject." *Prime v. Prime*, 172 Or. 34, 139 P.2d 550, 557 (1943). The IRS argued that the above quotation was dicta, apparently because it had been described as such in *Fithian v. United States*, 45 F. App'x 700, 701 (9th Cir. 2002). But *Fithian* was unpublished and lacked precedential value. Even worse, it was decided before January 1, 2007, when the Ninth Circuit began allowing citation of unpublished opinions. See 9th Cir. R. 36-3(a), (c). Thus, not only was *Fithian* not controlling, it could not even properly be cited. The payments at issue terminated upon the wife's death and the husband was allowed to take an alimony deduction.

e. **Comment:** The IRS's argument against the deduction was uncommonly weak. But the IRS is run by tax experts, not by family law experts.

f. **Lesson:** Do not take the risk that the IRS will misread the law of your state and disallow an alimony deduction. If you intend that payments be deductible as alimony, state directly in the decree or agreement that the payments terminate upon death.

# CHAPTER 4

## Premarital Agreements

### ■■ GENERAL OVERVIEW

There are many reasons to do a premarital agreement. A premarital agreement in North Carolina is a written contract between a prospective bride and prospective groom that outlines their mutually agreed expectations and rights, generally upon either divorce or the death of a spouse during marriage. A premarital agreement allows the prospective bride and prospective groom to control and design their own destinies in the event of divorce or death.

Persons who are on second marriages are frequently candidates for premarital agreements. Many times, there are children from earlier marriages, and perhaps estate planning for these children needs to be done with the help of a premarital agreement. You see, North Carolina law defines an elective share your spouse receives at death if your will does not provide at least that much for the surviving spouse. For example, if you want property you had on the date of marriage to your second spouse to go to your children from a prior marriage, then you might look at a premarital agreement.

A divorce with its accompanying equitable distribution of property can reap absolute havoc for the family business. In a premarital agreement, both active and passive appreciation of a family business can be waived.

If you want to be in charge of your own financial destiny in the event of a divorce or death, a premarital agreement is the way to go.

## SHOULD I GET A PREMARITAL AGREEMENT?

Dear Carolyn:

I am considering getting married. I have found the love of my life, except there is one problem. I am not sure we view money and credit cards the same way. I am conservative, and I pay my credit cards off every month. I believe in balancing the monthly budget with the income I earn. I even save in my 401(k) and set aside some money for emergencies. My potential bride-to-be is always behind on her credit cards, and she spends everything she makes, and more if there is a credit card available. Should I get a premarital agreement? What should I do?

*Money Concerns*

Carolyn Answers ...

Dear Money Concerns,

You might want to run—not walk—away, from this potential bride! Money fights and problems are the number one cause of divorce in my experience, followed by adultery (sex) and substance abuse issues. In support of my theory, a Citibank survey indicated that 57 percent of divorcing couples cited money as the primary disagreement leading to the divorce. While this may seem weird, one of the similarities persons entering into relationships should have are similar FICO scores.

You need frank and open discussions with your lady before it gets too serious between you. In these discussions, you need to talk about the use of the future family money. How will bills be handled? How will savings and emergency funds be accumulated? Will there be a joint checking and savings account? Will you consider filing joint tax returns?

Perhaps your potential bride can be educated, or perhaps there was one life event that tipped her over the credit edge. Or, perhaps the debt is education loans which plague many of our millennials. Thinking someone will change if you enter the relationship is usually foolish, but you can see if she can be re-educated.

A common way of dividing bills among partners, both of whom are wage earners of approximately the same amount of income, is a proportional sharing of household bills. Let's say, for example, you have 60 percent of the after-tax income, and she has 40 percent of the after-tax income. Let's also say the household bills with rent or a mortgage are $4,000 per month. You should place 60 percent of $4,000 in the household account, which is $2,400. She should place $1,600 in the household account. Each of you can retain the leftover money for individual expenses, such as clothing, nails, and fashion magazines (or whatever). The plan should be for credit cards to be paid off monthly. You also need to have a savings plan that would provide for 3 months of emergency money, which, in my example, would be $12,000.

And, yes, get a premarital agreement!

Carolyn Blogs On ...

## PLANNING FOR YOUR FUTURE "FORMER" SPOUSE

The North Carolina Premarital Agreement Act describes the law for the creation of valid, enforceable premarital agreements. The North Carolina Premarital Agreement Act is under North Carolina General Statutes Chapter 52B.

**Formalities:** Obviously, a premarital agreement should be completed before the wedding, and practically, I suggest the prenuptial agreement be finalized before the wedding invitations are sent out. The agreement must be in writing and signed by both parties. Note, the statute does not require notarization, but I think it is a better practice to notarize the premarital agreement. I also ask my clients to initial and date each page so no one can argue later than a page was changed or slip-sheeted into the document. (Yes, I do this every day, and I have seen this slip-sheet argument of "that is not what I signed.")

**Content:** The content of a North Carolina premarital agreement varies based upon individual needs and wants. Most typically, content revolves around three topics: spousal support, property division (equitable distribution) upon divorce, and death (wills and trusts).

**Spousal support** is easiest to discuss. The parties to the marriage can decide ahead of time exactly how spousal support should be handled at divorce, or even whether there should be spousal support. Spousal support can be waived in the premarital agreement. Likewise, spousal support can be a stated amount dependent on the number of years of marriage before separation/divorce. Spousal support can be anything you want it to be, as long as you agree before the wedding in the prenupt.

**Property Division** or Equitable Distribution can be waived in its entirety. Or in the alternative, parameters for the division of property in the event of a divorce can be put in place. For example, the bride and groom could agree to let the title to assets control in the event of a separation. For example, the prenupt can provide: if husband puts wife's name on real estate, that real estate becomes hers in the event of the divorce because the real estate was titled to her. Important many times for family businesses are premarital provisions defining the right of the nonfamily member to the business or its appreciation in the event of separation and divorce.

Marriage creates by law rights and obligations upon the death of the surviving spouse to the deceased spouse's **estate**. These obligations, rights, and benefits can be altered by a premarital agreement. A prospective spouse can waive the rights to a future surviving spouse's estate. (One can waive the right to take under the will of the future spouse.) In contrast, a prospective spouse can agree to alter the default provisions in the law to the future surviving spouse's estate.

The **support of a child** cannot be "adversely affected" by a premarital agreement.

One can decide which state's law applies to a premarital agreement, but I rarely see couples negotiating situs except when the prospective bride and groom are not from the same state, or the couple plans to move shortly after the wedding. I have, on rare occasion, seen forum shopping to get away from Community Property states.

Carolyn Blogs On ...

## PARENTS, CHILDREN, AND PREMARITAL AGREEMENTS

This post is directed at parents who have worked hard enough, and been fortunate enough, to accumulate significant property. You desire, naturally enough, to leave that property to your children. But you do not want that property to pass to your children's spouses. How can this goal be accomplished?

Understand initially that you may not need any special measures. When a marriage ends in divorce, most states give special treatment to property acquired by gift or inheritance. In North Carolina, gifts and inheritances are defined as separate property that the court lacks the power to divide. N.C. Gen. Stat. ("G.S.") § 50-20. Separate property includes not only the initial amount of the gift or inheritance, but also any future "passive appreciation" in that gift or inheritance—growth caused by market forces, and not by the funds or efforts of your children after they are married.

For example, assume you have investment stock, bonds, or a bank account. If by gift or devise, you transfer this property to your children, the property transferred will be separate property. Any future passive appreciation in the gift or devise will be separate property also. Upon divorce, your child's spouse will not have any claim to separate property.

A special situation is presented, however, when you wish to make a gift or devise of an interest in a **business** in which your child works. The base value of such a gift or devise would be separate property. But any future growth would be marital property to the extent it is "active appreciation"—appreciation caused by your child's efforts. If your child works for the company, your child will probably cause at least some of the growth. If your child runs the company, your child may cause most or all of the growth. In this situation, there is a valid basis for taking special measures to protect the future growth in the company from being shared with your child's spouse.

What sort of special measures can you take?

To begin with, you can suggest to your child that your child enter into a premarital agreement with his or her spouse. The agreement can waive any marital interest in the growth of the company.

Be aware, however, that your child has valid reasons not to sign such an agreement. Attitudes toward premarital agreements vary, and some people prefer not to sign them. In particular, some people still adhere to the traditional view that married persons should share everything. If your child is not willing to sign a premarital agreement, you cannot force them to do so.

Even if your child is willing to sign an agreement, your child's spouse may not be willing. The law normally requires married persons to share income earned during the marriage. The reason active appreciation is marital property is that it is very easy for owners of businesses to pay themselves little or no salary, and take their compensation in the form of appreciation in the value of the business. If a premarital agreement waives the marital interest in active appreciation, the effect may be to frustrate your child's spouse's right to share in your child's earnings during the marriage.

With divorce rates near 50 percent, your child's spouse needs to protect his or her financial security in the event of divorce, especially if your child has children. It is reasonable to raise the possibility of a premarital agreement, but you should not necessarily expect that your child will be willing or able to sign one.

Carolyn Blogs On ...

### GRAY MARRIAGE–PLAN WISELY!

By now, everyone in North Carolina has probably heard that Sharon and Ozzy Osbourne are most likely divorcing after 33 years of marriage. There has been an upturn in so-called "gray divorces"—where a couple divorces after the age of 50. But, with gray divorces also come gray marriages!

Gray marriages are defined differently by different people, but generally, persons over 50 who remarry may be considered gray marriages. Others don't consider a marriage to be "gray" until at least one of the spouses is 60 or older. Here are my topmost concerns for "gray marriages"—marriages for people over 50. You should go through each of these points, many of which can be handled in **prenuptial agreement**.

1. **Medical and Other Basic** Necessaries: Husband and wife are financially responsible for each other's necessaries, such as medical, housing, and basic food. Common wisdom is that you cannot necessarily contract around this Doctrine of Necessaries in a premarital agreement because the providers, particularly the medical providers, are not parties to the premarital agreement. In my opinion, it is helpful in a premarital agreement (if the parties want the provision) to require the prospective bride and groom to put the Waiver of Medical Necessaries on file with all healthcare providers. It, at least, gives the provider notice that the other spouse may contest liability for necessaries. Health care, while potentially expensive at any time in life, can become very expensive as we age. Is this potential medical commitment one you are willing to take on? Of course, I've seen divorces happen over this issue of medical necessaries alone

in persons in their 80s in order to preserve assets for estate planning. This is tough stuff.

2. **Wills and Estate:** How will the marriage affect your will and your estate planning? If you predecease your new spouse without a waiver of estate rights in your premarital agreement, your new spouse will get a percentage of your estate established by North Carolina law. Adult "children" often become contentious and unsupportive of Mom's new squeeze, if these adult "children" feel "Mom's new husband will steal what they are entitled to." As if this is not Mom's money to do what she wants to do with it—LOL

3. **Living Arrangements:** Will you establish a new household together after the wedding, or will the new couple be moving into one or the other's already established home? If possible and financially feasible, I suggest starting over "fresh" with a new residence for both of you together—one you jointly establish. Why? The spouse moving in the pre-existing home frequently complains that the residence doesn't really "belong" to him/her, particularly if that spouse doesn't have his/her name on the deed. And, pre-existing residences can have the bad karma of a previous relationship, or even too many uncomfortable recollections if the spouse lost a prior or former spouse by death while living in the pre-existing residence. If your legal name is not on the deed to the home, then your household furnishings that you move into the residence will likely not be covered by the homeowner's insurance if a disaster happens, such as a tornado, flood, fire, or hurricane. If you move into a pre-existing residence deeded to the other partner only, will you suddenly have to move out if your partner dies? This needs to be covered in a premarital agreement, if at all possible.

4. **Income Tax Returns:** The government always has to be there in your marriage as a third party, like it or not. Will your partner and you, after the marriage, file joint federal income tax returns? Will this have a hefty price tag? How will you allocate the taxes between you and your new spouse? If your legal name is not on the Promissory Note and Deed of Trust on this home, then you cannot deduct the mortgage interest, even if you are paying half (or even more) of the mortgage payment. The marriage penalty is alive and well, and quite costly in certain instances.

If you are contemplating marriage, you might have your CPA run some pro forma tax returns. If both the bride- and groom-to-be are in the 28 percent federal tax bracket, the combined taxable income could cause extra income taxes, frequently called the marriage penalty.

5. **Income Discrepancy:** If one partner is high net worth and the other partner is low net worth, you as a couple can potentially make use of the unlimited marital deduction twice under current law, and that certainly could be an estate tax saving worth the wedding.
6. **Social Security:** If you were married to your former spouse for the required 10 years, your Social Security should be evaluated based upon your first spouse's Social Security earnings record unless you remarry. If you remarry, you do not retain the Social Security benefits related to your first marriage partner.
7. **Spousal Support:** Are you receiving alimony from your previous spouse? If so, you will most likely lose that payment.
8. Have a CPA evaluate the total cost of the marriage and not just the cost of the wedding party. You might be surprised. At least, you should know.

Carolyn Blogs On ...

## ▚ PROCEDURES FOR SIGNING

Premarital agreements are favored by modern law, but only when they were signed using procedures that the court sees as fair.

How do the courts define a fair procedure? Three factors are important. First, the parties must sign voluntarily and not under unreasonable pressure. To take an extreme example, a premarital agreement signed under a threat of physical violence would certainly be invalid for duress. Other improper acts include threats to falsely accuse a spouse of a crime or to interfere with a spouse's immigration status.

Threats make an agreement procedurally unfair only if the threats are improper. One recurring issue has been whether the agreement is procedurally unfair if one spouse threatens not to marry the other unless an agreement is signed. But no one is required to marry anyone. A threat to cancel an engagement unless a premarital agreement is signed is therefore generally not viewed as wrongful.

Second, while the parties must be free to make a voluntary decision whether to sign the agreement, the power to make a voluntary decision does not mean much if a spouse lacks access to relevant information. In particular, since almost all premarital agreements require the parties to give up rights in one another's property, it is essential that each party has a reasonably accurate understanding of how much property the other owns.

It is not absolutely necessary that the couple engages in financial disclosure. Actual knowledge of the other spouse's assets, from any source, is sufficient to avoid procedural unfairness. But disputes over knowledge tend to turn into "he said/she said" issues over who knew what, and judges will sometimes find a lack of knowledge in these cases, especially if the agreement is substantively unfair.

A better approach is to include, as appendices to a premarital agreement, full disclosure by both parties of their assets and incomes. When financial disclosure is attached to the agreement, it is clear to everyone that both spouses had sufficient financial information to make an informed and voluntary decision whether to sign the agreement.

Third, even if a spouse is free to make a voluntary decision and has full knowledge of the relevant financial facts, a spouse must also have full knowledge of what his or her rights would be without the agreement. These rights are not common knowledge. The best way to ensure that both parties know the relevant law is to make certain that both parties are represented by attorneys. Representation by attorneys is also a good way to avoid other problems, as spouses who are represented by counsel are less likely to be influenced by improper threats or pressure.

It is not absolutely necessary that both parties have counsel. In particular, if a spouse is advised to retain counsel and refuses, the refusal does not prevent the parties from signing an agreement. Courts are reluctant to allow a party who refused to obtain counsel to claim ignorance of the law. But again, questions about whether a spouse was advised to seek counsel tend to turn into unpredictable "he said/she said" disagreements. The prudent option, when a spouse does not have counsel, is to state expressly in the agreement that the spouse was directly advised to retain counsel and voluntarily chose not to do so.

To summarize, if you are the spouse who desires an enforceable premarital agreement, there are three basic procedural requirements. You must avoid improper threats or pressure, you must disclose your assets and income in a form you can later prove (ideally in an appendix to the agreement), and you must make certain that your future spouse has counsel (or at the worst, expressly waives counsel in the agreement).

Carolyn Blogs On ...

### ▪▪ MY FIANCÉ WANTS A PRENUPT—I DON'T WANT TO SIGN!

A premarital agreement, of course, requires the consent of both future spouses. Sometimes future spouses will disagree about whether to sign a premarital agreement.

Understand initially that this is a very serious issue that will affect your life forever. The decisions you make regarding this agreement will play a very important role, possibly even a critical role, in determining your financial future.

Many future spouses, especially women, when confronted with a strong request for a premarital agreement, have swallowed their reservations and signed it. Years later, they discover that the effect of the agreement is to allow their spouse to leave the marriage at any time, leaving them with no property and no spousal support. Few decisions have been regretted as intensely as the decision to sign a substantively unfair premarital agreement.

Your financial future is your responsibility. You are not required to sign any premarital agreement. While many couples have such agreements, many couples also do not. You have the power to accept the famous advice of former First Lady Nancy Reagan: "Just Say No."

You should also recognize that decisions regarding this agreement are too important to be made without assistance. You need to know what your rights would be without the agreement. You need to know the value of your future spouse's property. You need to know what the agreement says. Do not lightly assume you know that; a trained lawyer can include provisions that seem meaningful but are actually worth nothing. An agreement to agree, for example, is not legally enforceable. You need the advice of an attorney to guide you in making decisions about the agreement.

"But if I don't sign the agreement," you may be thinking, "my future spouse won't marry me!" It may seem so when you are in love, but marrying this particular person is not the central question in the universe. Many future spouses have said, "I must marry this person!" and signed an unfair agreement that they later deeply regretted.

If your future spouse is insisting that you must give up all future financial security as a condition of the marriage, you need to consider very carefully whether you really want to marry this person. **Divorce** rates are close to 50 percent. It is very foreseeable that your marriage will not last forever. You are responsible for your own financial future.

While signing an unfair agreement can be a complete financial disaster, it is also important not to assume blindly that the agreement is unfair. There are valid reasons why future spouses want premarital agreements. Try to find out why your future spouse wants one.

Then consider whether your future spouse's needs can be met without unreasonably sacrificing your future financial security. For instance, you and your spouse both are employed; you may be able to provide for your own future security. If your spouse is wealthy, the agreement may give you a reasonable financial future even if you are not getting 50 percent of everything.

Be aware of the issue of children. Discuss this issue with your spouse. If you do not intend to have children, be aware of the possibility that your views on this question might change as you get older. If you intend to stay home with any children you have, be aware that however good that decision may be for children, it will limit your future earnings. The law gives you rights to property division and alimony that are intended, in material part, as compensation for the time spent out of the workplace raising children. Consider carefully whether you want to give up these rights.

The bottom line is: There are good reasons why the law requires property division when a marriage ends in death or divorce, and support when a marriage ends in divorce. Be careful before signing a complete waiver of these rights. It may be a decision you will ultimately regret.

# CHAPTER 5

## Divorce

### ▚ GENERAL OVERVIEW

In North Carolina, an absolute divorce is almost always obtained on the basis of a 1-year separation. Once you and your spouse have lived continuously apart for 1 year, without resuming the marital relationship, either of you may obtain an absolute divorce. Attempts at reconciliation marked by isolated instances of sexual intercourse will not automatically end the period of continuous separation. However, instances of sexual intercourse and nights spent together may add to the totality of circumstances sufficient to cause a court to find that you have voluntarily renewed the marital relationship. Should a court so find, the 12-month clock will be reset.

### ▚ GROUNDS FOR DIVORCE

Dear Carolyn:

    My spouse has done something that is terribly embarrassing to me. It also might be criminal. Everyone in the community knows; our friends know, and I am mortified and humiliated. I want a divorce. Do I have grounds for getting a divorce?

*Humiliated*

Carolyn Answers ...

Dear Humiliated,

Assuming both spouses are sane, the only "ground" for a North Carolina divorce is 365 days of separation. Separation means to live in separate residences and to hold yourself out as separated. Only one party to the marriage has to formulate the intent to live separate and apart forever. So, the embarrassing event is not a technical element to the North Carolina divorce. After the required 365 days of living separate and apart, with the intent to remain separated, you may apply to the court for your divorce.

The embarrassing event is important to your emotional decision to seek a divorce. I would take the time to make the choice, particularly since it seems you are talking about one bad act, rather than a pattern of conduct. Give yourself some time to heal. Perhaps obtaining some counseling with a psychologist and speak to your minister.

Since I do not know what "bad act" your spouse committed, I tried to think of an analogous situation. Cecil the Lion comes to mind. What should the wife of Dr. Walter Palmer do? Dentist Palmer killed the beloved Cecil the Lion in July 2015 in Zimbabwe. Cecil was a tagged lion in a study being done by Oxford University, and he lived in a park. Neighbors describe Ms. Palmer as a quiet person. Should she leave him over this rather international debacle? Certainly, there is public humiliation. He has referred his patients to other dentists, so it seems he has lost his dental practice, presumably marital or community property. Apparently, he was convicted earlier of poaching a black bear. He has fishing license violations. He has sexual harassment in his background. He may be leaving her because he may be going to jail. From an emotional point of view, Ms. Palmer has a difficult decision to make on whether to divorce or stand by Dr. Palmer.

You, like Mrs. Palmer, may find yourself in a grieving process, and the first thing that may happen to you is denial, disbelief that this is happening to me. Then you may experience anger. The phase after anger is complacency, an "I don't care" response. Finally, you will achieve normalcy. Get a counselor to help you understand where you are in the healing process and how to factor in where you are in the healing process for good decision making.

Dear Carolyn:

My wife just lost her mother about 6 months ago, but she cannot seem to get over it and get on with life. She is not taking care of herself or our children. She seems tired all of the time, and cannot seem to concentrate on any task. She is drinking more, and I am afraid for her to be driving the children. I am thinking about divorce at this point to protect the children. What do you think is going on here? How will the court look at divorce under my circumstances?

*Concerned*

Carolyn Answers ...

Dear Concerned,

Your wife needs help from a licensed psychologist for what appears to me as an experienced divorce attorney to be depression. Depression is a serious medical problem and so very commonly the cause of divorce. You should facilitate her getting the mental health help that she needs, just like you would if your wife had any other medical problem. On occasion, a spouse refuses medical/mental health help, and the other spouse's life becomes miserable and intolerable; in that event of refusal of help, divorce may be appropriate.

You can share with your wife that depression is common, and luckily, many celebrities have been willing to talk about their depression. Angelina Jolie reports she went to a very dark place after her mother died, much like your wife. Jolie used physical exercise to shake the depression. Lady Gaga once said: "I'm lucky I found one little glimmer stored away." Gwyneth Paltrow disclosed: "I felt like a zombie." Eva Longoria opened up on Dr. Oz about post-divorce struggles with depression.

The following are some of the red flags of depression, and your wife has many of these red flags. Eight commons factors that suggest depression and the need for a psychologist are as follows: (1) Tired all the time; (2) Hopelessness or helplessness; (3) Loss of interest in daily activities; (4) Changes in sleeping and/or eating habits; (5) Loss of concentration; (6) Negative thoughts out of control; (7) Changes in mood; (8) Increased use of alcohol or other reckless behavior.

As I understand it, there are three "treatment" considerations for typical depression: First, physical activity can elevate your mood. Second, therapy with a psychologist can help. Finally, medications for depression exist. Good luck in getting your wife help, and let me know how your situation progresses.

## DIVORCE OF BED AND BOARD: SNEAK ATTACK!

Dear Carolyn:

I live in North Carolina, but I went to Oklahoma hunting with buddies. While there, I was served with Divorce from Bed and Board papers. I came home, and the house was empty. I wasn't expecting this. She took our children, and she is gone. I wasn't even left with a towel. The bank accounts are empty. I have no furniture. What should I do?

*Worried and in the Dark*

Carolyn Answers ...

Dear Worried and in the Dark,

This is always a tough decision, and the law that applies to this is called: "Innocent Spouse Relief." There are some things that you need to know in making the critical decision of whether to file a joint income tax return with your spouse.

First, you need to know that you do not have to sign a joint return, but if you elect to do so, you are potentially 100 percent liable for any income taxes, interest, or penalties related to the return you sign. Yes, I said **100 percent**, not 50 percent. You see, the Internal Revenue Code holds each signer of a tax return jointly and severally liable for all taxes, interest, and penalties, absent a cosigner being an innocent spouse. So, to me, signing a joint tax return is always a big decision for a person with a small business. Contrast this with spouses who both have W-2 incomes from employment with third parties; if the only income on the return is W-2 income, then generally, it is safe to sign a joint return properly prepared. You, however, are in the riskier situation with the small business.

Second, don't assume that you will be granted innocent spouse status with the IRS just because you don't know much about the tax return.

There are many, many factors the IRS considers in whether to grant innocent spouse status to a person in your position. Note, it is easier to obtain innocent spouse treatment if you are separated or divorced because there are different innocent spouse standards applied to those who are divorced, as contrasted with persons married and living together.

You might Google IRS Form 8857, which is the form you file for Innocent Spouse Relief. Read through the form and look at the factors considered. There are many factors, but a few are the following:

First, the IRS considers your lifestyle as contrasted with the amount reported on the return. For example, if you are living in a big, expensive home and driving new cars and reporting $20,000 on the tax return, you need to find out where the money is coming from for this lifestyle that you are currently living and spending. The IRS expects that you make a reasonable inquiry. You need to require that you receive copies of any return you sign. Your tax return preparer must also give you copies of your returns for a reasonable copy charge.

Another factor the IRS will review is whether you have been a victim of domestic violence. One area of domestic abuse is financial control and oppression. While this will not likely get you a 50B domestic violence protective order in domestic courts, financial oppression is reviewed carefully by the IRS.

As a final consideration, whatever unpaid taxes are owed for 2013 will be a marital debt in your equitable distribution (property settlement); therefore, this is one factor going in your favor of filing a joint return, which is usually the least expensive filing status.

I would recommend that you consult with a family lawyer and with a CPA or lawyer skilled in Innocent Spouse Relief. Filing a joint return can be a very big decision. Likely the return is extended until October 15, so you still have some time to carefully research your options. Good luck!

## DO-IT-YOURSELF-DIVORCE ADVICE

Dear Carolyn:

I am in need of an uncontested divorce. I have been married 13 years but have not seen my husband for 8 years. I know he lives somewhere in Fort Lauderdale. I also know his last employer … nothing much else.

He has a Facebook account, where I requested his address, and he will not reply.

At any rate, I have stage IV lung cancer and need this divorce as soon as possible. I went to the county Web site and pulled down the "do-it-yourself" version and found it very confusing since I do not have a specific address.

Question: Do you or someone you know, take payments for an uncontested divorce? Do you know of anyone who could help me even with the "do-it-yourself" version?

*Do It Yourself*

Carolyn Answers ...

Dear Do It Yourself,

I am sorry for your situation, and I wish you the best with your health and battle with cancer. This is tough!!! and sad!!!

You need to find his address in Florida if you want to do this yourself; otherwise, there are a lot of legal steps regarding the service of the divorce complaint under Rule 4 of the Rules of Civil Procedure. If you cannot find the address, you need the help of an attorney.

Now, to finding his address:

If I were looking for his address, I would start with an Apex Background Check at *www.apexbackgroundcheck.net*. You will have to open an account, but there is no charge for opening the account. A search in Florida will cost $22; you will need his first name, last name, date of birth, and gender.

Also, there are many public record sources of addresses. The next place I would look is the Land Records and Deeds in Florida. The Broward County records on real estate are public. The third place I would look would be the Department of Highway Safety and Motor Vehicles. He probably has a driver's license and/or a car: both of these would have his current address. If you cannot do this research yourself, a private detective in Broward County, Florida, would likely be cheaper than an attorney in finding your estranged husband's address. With the address, you can do the "do-it-yourself" divorce you want to do. Keep in mind that divorce cuts off all of your claims against your estranged husband, including property division and alimony.

Two possible legal options for free services for you are Legal Aid and the Elon Law School Elder Law Clinic. I do not know how old you are, but if you are age 60 and above, you may qualify for Elon Law School's Elder Law Clinic, which handles civil legal issues; a divorce is a civil legal issue. There is also a monthly income qualifier and since you are married, that income qualifier is $2,200 per month or less. Given your compelling health issue, I hope that the Elder Law Clinic will help you. The phone is 336-279-9314, and the e-mail is *elderlaw@elon.edu*.

North Carolina has a doctrine of medical necessaries, so he really should want to divorce as the hospitals can go after him for your medical bills. You might tell him that through Facebook. The hospitals *will* find him ... On the other hand, he can contest your estate.

If these suggestions do not solve your problem, please write again, and I will look for other solutions for you. If you write again, include your age and your approximate monthly income, as many low-cost solutions have qualifiers. Take care ...

## BASIC DIVORCE PROCEDURE IN NC

Dear Carolyn:

My husband wants a divorce, and I agree, and we don't need a lawyer because we don't have kids or property, or even shared money. The only thing we have together, property-wise, we've both agreed he will keep. I have all my divorce papers, I just haven't filled them out. I was told to do it in front of a notary. Do I have to fill them out in front of one, or can I take it to one once they're already filled out? And after that, what can they do? Just sign it or do they file it? That's where I'm confused.

*Confused*

Carolyn Answers ...

Dear Confused,

A divorce can be a little more complex with regard to paperwork than perhaps it should be. I'll give you some DIY guidance after answering your question about a notary. Simply, concerning the notary, the notary only needs to see you sign. You should have identification with you as the notary will need to confirm who you are. You should already have the forms completed, EXCEPT FOR YOUR SIGNATURE, when you approach the notary. The notary will watch you sign and attach the notary affidavit and seal. You can find a notary at your bank.

You will then need to go to the clerk of court in the county where you live and file the divorce complaint. The next step is service of your husband with the complaint and summons (the clerk gives you the summons). You can pay and have the sheriff serve him, or send him a certified mail copy of the complaint and summons. Or, since this seems friendly, he could file a paper with the clerk stating that he has received the complaint and that he wants the divorce also. The clerk can then help you get a date for the divorce and fill out the Bureau of Vital Statistics paperwork.

Keep in mind that an absolute divorce cuts off ALL rights to property and spousal support. You might want to pull a joint credit report and make sure you know whether your husband signed you up for any debts you did not know about. Enjoy your new life and write again if you have further questions.

## PROTECTING YOUR CREDIT

Dear Carolyn:

I am going through a divorce, and I am afraid my ex may have taken out credit cards in my name. What can I do?

*Afraid*

Carolyn Answers ...

Dear Afraid,

I generally tell divorce clients to obtain two credit reports, both of which can be legally obtained: 1) the client's personal credit report and 2) the client's joint credit report with the ex-spouse. Factually, you should be able to determine from the credit reports whether there are credit cards in your name that you do not know about.

There are generally three credit reporting companies: Equifax, Experian, and Transamerica. Once a year, each of these companies will give you a free credit report, and quite frankly, you should check every year for the rest of your life. An alternative would be to subscribe to a service that provides credit monitoring.

If you are the parent of a minor child, with a close name to that of your ex, you might also check your child's credit report if you are the parent with legal custody or joint legal custody. I have seen many situations where a parent has obtained credit by stealing the identity of a child with a very similar name: such as Fred or Fred, Jr.

If you find problems with the credit reports when you receive them, please take immediate action. Go over the reports with your divorce attorney. Write any letters for your credit file with the credit bureaus that are needed, and cancel cards that you did not apply for with an explanation. If there are balances on the cards in your name, and you did not incur the balances, discuss with your attorney how to get the culprit who stole your credit.

# CHAPTER 6

## Divorce Recovery

### ■■ GENERAL OVERVIEW

A topic dear to my heart is divorce recovery. I have personally experienced it, and I am empathic to each troubled soul that walks into my office. You can be okay after a divorce and happier than ever. I am.

You need to understand that divorce is a grieving process. You go through the stages of denial, anger, complacency, and back to normalcy. Frequently, you and your ex are at different stages in this process, making settlements sometimes harder. You can get stuck in a stage, such as the stage of anger. Seek counseling with a psychologist to help combat the risk of getting stuck. It seems some never get over a divorce, and most likely, they are simply stuck in a stage of the grieving process.

Find new interests if you are going through a divorce, and I'm not necessarily talking about rebounding into a new relationship. Learn something you have always wanted to learn. Travel to a place you have always wanted to go, but didn't. Read something new. Shopping therapy is good, if reasonable. Don't sit in the muck. Live, learn, and breathe.

## ▚ BACK IN THE SADDLE

Dear Carolyn:

I am a recently divorced female and age 64. Am I too old to find a new relationship? If not, do you have any suggestions for finding someone appropriate to date?

64

Carolyn Answers ...

Dear 64,

You are certainly not alone at age 64 finding yourself "divorced." In the last 2 decades, the divorce of persons over 50 has doubled, and more surprisingly, has doubled in the "gray divorce" area of over 65. Further, the male to female ratio in the 55- to 64-year-old age group is 92 men for every 100 women; not bad odds.

Your best place to find someone to date is "right in front" of you in an activity you already enjoy, such as church, a club, or sport. That being said, I am a big believer of reinventing yourself as part of the divorce recovery process. So, I suggest you make a bucket list of activities you would like to try and start trying them. There are some activities that seem to be dominated by men, so you might pick a few of those that you enjoy. For example, I believe you will find more eligible men in flying clubs, off-roading clubs, skiing, and golf. Step outside of your "box" or "rut."

I frequently am asked about the online match services. While I have occasionally had good reports, I have had seriously bad reports. There are large numbers of people in your age group seeking matches online. One of the popular online match services has had a 300 percent growth rate since 2000.

Here are some rules for dating someone you just met, or you met online.

1. Do not give out your address at the outset. Meet in a public place, such as a well-populated restaurant.
2. Tell someone you trust where you are going and when you plan to return home.

3. As soon as possible, do a thorough background check on the person. A private detective might help you with a background search. If the individual has not always lived in North Carolina, do a multistate background search. Also, check the sex offender list, but keep in mind the list didn't start until January 1, 1996.

4. Do not introduce the date to your grandchildren or other minors until you are sure about the background of the date. Above all, do not let the date keep your grandchildren unsupervised until a thorough background check has been done. Even then, exercise caution with minors. Chances are the person you will date at your age will have been in other relationships. If there is a divorce file, go to the courthouse and read it. While you are at the courthouse, look to see if there are any 50B (domestic violence) protective orders in the person's past.

5. Protect your "identity" information, such as your Social Security number, passwords, and financial information.

6. Have fun, but take care.

## SECOND-MARRIAGE CONSIDERATIONS

Dear Carolyn:

I am a 55-year-old woman, and I am thinking about getting married again. I was married to my first husband 20 years. I re-entered the workforce about 10 years ago. I have two adult children and a grandchild. What considerations do I have?

55

Carolyn Answers ...

Dear 55,

Here are Carolyn's top seven concerns for "gray marriages"—marriages for people over 50. You should go through each of these issues, many of which can be handled in a premarital agreement.

1. The doctrine of necessaries: Spouses are financially responsible for each other's medical necessaries. The concern here is, as we age,

health care can become very expensive. Is this a commitment you are willing to make? Of course, I've seen divorces happen over this issue of medical necessaries alone in persons in their 80s to preserve assets for estate planning.

2. Will the marriage disrupt your estate plan? Your new spouse will have rights to a portion of your estate unless those rights are waived in a premarital agreement. Adult children, many times, become quite anxious if they feel "mom's new love will steal their inheritance."

3. Will you create a new home together, or will you be moving into one or the other's existing home? I recommend starting over "fresh" with a new home for both of you. Why? The partner moving in the existing home frequently feels that the home doesn't really belong to him/her. And, existing homes can have bad memories of a prior relationship in the home, or even too many sad memories if the partner lost a spouse by death while living in the existing home. If your name is not on the home, your furnishings that you bring into the home will likely not be covered by the homeowner's insurance if something happens like fire or flood. If you move into an existing home titled to the other spouse only, will you suddenly have to move out if your spouse dies?

4. Will you file joint income tax returns? Will this cost you more? If your name is not on the mortgage of an existing home, you cannot deduct the interest, even if you are paying half the payment. The marriage penalty is stiff and expensive. If you and your groom-to-be are both in the 28 percent tax bracket, your combined income could trigger extra taxes, frequently called the marriage penalty.

5. If you are high net worth, making use of the unlimited marital deduction in estate planning can be beneficial.

6. You will lose Social Security benefits related to your first spouse. You were married to your first spouse for the required 10 years, so you are entitled to have your Social Security evaluated based upon your first husband's earnings record unless you remarry.

7. If you are receiving alimony from your first husband, you will most likely lose that alimony.

## SURVIVING THE HOLIDAYS

Dear Carolyn:

I am a mom. I do not live with the father of my child. I have to admit I hate him, and the holidays do not make it easier. My child is 5, and a beautiful little girl. Help with surviving this holiday.

*Help*

Carolyn Answers ...

Dear Help,

Holidays are stressful. Holidays can be a time of depression for that "lost vision of the perfect family." I have a list of tips that I share with my clients.

1. Acknowledge how you feel. You are there in that you are admitting you hate the father. Now, mind you, it is not good that you hate the father, but at least you are acknowledging this problem. You might get some counseling sessions to deal with your situation.
2. Plan ahead, and then be flexible. Go over the holiday events with your child. You can even ask her what she wants for gifts and activities, but you make the final decision. Do something one-on-one with your daughter that she enjoys. It might be a special movie or the reindeer at a petting zoo, but create a special memory, and then document it with photos in an album or a video.
3. Custody orders vary in degree of specificity regarding the holiday schedule, exchange times, and exchange locations. I hope yours has exactness to it, with a clause that says the parents can agree in writing (e-mail) to vary from the court order.
4. Communicate with the other parent regarding both activities and gifts for your child, if at all possible. Hopefully, both of you will spend approximately the same amount of money and not try to outdo the other. Talking with the father will also give assurance that the child gets different gifts from each parent. If you want to do an event, such as Holiday on Ice, advise your ex, so, hopefully, he will select another event. The child probably won't want to sit through Holiday on Ice twice.

5. Finally, since you hate your ex, do not buy a gift for the child to take to Dad's house that gets even with Dad. I know it might be tempting to buy your daughter a kitten, but if Dad is allergic to cats, this gift isn't going to work well.

## ▍▍ DIVORCE RECOVERY TIP

Seek peace. When I think of peace, the words of an old hymn come to mind:

> *"When peace, like a river, attendeth my way,*
> *When sorrows like sea billows roll;*
> *Whatever my lot, Thou has taught me to say,*
> *It is well, it is well, with my soul."*

# CHAPTER 7

## Domestic Violence

### ▰ GENERAL OVERVIEW

**"50B": Domestic Violence Protection Order, known as a Chapter 50B under the North Carolina General Statutes**

**1. What is a Domestic Violence Protection Order or "50B"?**

Any North Carolina resident has the right to file for a Domestic Violence Protection Order, known as a "50B." A 50B provides protection from someone you have a current personal relationship with or have had a personal relationship with who does or has done any of the following to you or your minor child:

- Attempts to cause bodily injury, or intentionally causing bodily injury; or
- Places you or a family member in fear of imminent serious bodily injury; or
- Continued harassment, as defined in G.S. 14-277.3A, that rises to such a level as to inflict substantial emotional distress; or
- Commits any rape or sexual offense that is defined in G.S. 14-27.2 through G.S. 14-27.7.

2. **How can a Domestic Violence Protection Order or "50B" protect me and my immediate family?**

   Depending on the facts of your case, the court has the right to take the following action (50B-3 Relief):
   - Provide you with a temporary order for custody of any minor children that shall not exceed 1 year and order the alleged abuser to pay temporary child support and establish temporary visitation and prohibit overnight visitation;
   - Tell the police to remove the alleged abuser from the home and help you to return to your home;
   - Order the alleged abuser to stay away from your home, the children's school, your workplace, friends' homes, or any place where you may be using as shelter;
   - Order the alleged abuser to pay temporary spousal support;
   - Order the alleged abuser to turn over any firearms and prohibit the alleged abuser from purchasing a firearm;
   - Order the alleged abuser to pay for attorney's fees;
   - Order the alleged abuser not to cruelly treat or abuse any animal owned, possessed, kept, or held as a pet by either party or by a minor child and/or give you possession of your pet;
   - Order the alleged abuser to do what you ask in court if the judge agrees.

3. **What if I am falsely accused of domestic violence?**

   You need to vigorously defend yourself and take the claim against you very seriously. You need to provide all the documentation and witnesses possible to support your innocence. Woodruff Family Law Group believes that a false accusation of domestic violence is a form of domestic abuse in and of itself.

   Woodruff Family Law Group and its staff continue to stand against any form of domestic violence and is an active business that annually supports Family Service of the Piedmont, Inc., Women's Resource Center and other organizations that stand against domestic violence.

## FACEBOOK THREATS

Dear Carolyn:

My ex is posting all kinds of things about me on Facebook. He calls me a slut and a whore. He doesn't even have privacy settings on his Facebook, so I fear that my (our) children who are ages 14 and 16 may somehow get access. He also said: "I hope I see my ex in a dark alley," which I take as a threat. How do I stop this? We have a custody case coming up in a couple of months.

*Needs to Stop*

Carolyn Answers ...

Dear Needs to Stop,

Facebook has many, many great aspects. I personally use Facebook, BUT I would NEVER say anything negative about anyone on Facebook. Facebook negativity is the ruin of relationships. No one involved in litigation should even remotely think about making a post about his/her case on Facebook. The North Carolina State Bar has advised attorneys to admonish clients not to post on social media regarding his/her case. Whatever you do, do not respond on Facebook to your ex's Facebook posts.

Next, you need to preserve the evidence. There are at least three steps you need to take:

1. First, have your attorney immediately write to the opposing attorney a letter requesting that all evidence, particularly social media evidence, be preserved. The letter is typically called a "spoliation of evidence" letter, or in other words, don't spoil the evidence.

2. Make copies of the posts, and give the copies to your attorney. You have these posts legally since there are no privacy settings on the Facebook page. If there were privacy settings, you could not use subterfuge in any way to obtain the information indirectly. With the privacy settings, a legitimate "friend" of your ex can provide the copies of the Facebook page or you can get the Facebook pages through a Request for Production of Documents.

3. I would also check other social media, such as Twitter. You may find more evidence.

Consider a 50B if you are actually physically frightened of him. The threat is there. A 50B is a domestic violence protective order. You can go to the Family Justice Center at 201 South Greene Street, Greensboro, for help with the 50B. The phone number for the Family Justice Center is 336-641-7233.

"I hope I see my ex in a dark alley." Is this the criminal act of communicating a threat? The United States Supreme Court recently reviewed the issue of threats on Facebook in *Elonis v. United States*. Facebook was not a party to the case.

Mr. Elonis made alleged threats against his ex-wife. The alleged threat: "There's one way to love you but a thousand ways to kill you. I'm not going to rest until your body is a mess, soaked in blood and dying from all the little cuts." His defense was that he was merely writing rap lyrics. Personally, I do not buy his argument, and this seems like a threat to me. The U.S. Supreme Court, however, threw out the conviction, and Chief Justice Roberts opined that it doesn't matter that a reasonable person would feel threatened. Roberts said that the Pennsylvania court had to determine if he actually intended to kill her and do all of these gross things to his ex. The court did not reach the issue of whether Mr. Elonis had the right under the First Amendment Freedom of Speech to say these things on Facebook.

Justice Clarence Thomas disagreed with the majority and thought the Facebook statements were "true threats." While I do not generally agree with Justice Thomas, I do on this occasion.

## CYBERSTALKING

Dear Carolyn:

I made the mistake of using an online dating service, meeting up with this guy, and then a second mistake of giving him my e-mail address. Now I cannot get rid of his harassing e-mails. He broke up with me by sending a terrible e-mail. He called me names, and he simply will not stop sending e-mails. I have asked him three times to stop. He then sent me an e-mail stating to be sure to take care of my dog's health and my health. I took this as a veiled threat. I'll bet if I counted he has sent me 100 e-mails or more since he broke up with me. What do I do?

*Desperate*

Carolyn Answers ...

Dear Desperate,

There are both legal and practical things you may want to do. Practically, do not let this go on as he is using this e-mailing to you as a form of control of you. He gets a sick pleasure knowing you are opening and reading his e-mails. Thus, you are thinking about him, right? So, let's first look at this proactively. I would discontinue the use of this particular e-mail account if at all possible. If, for some reason, you feel you cannot close the e-mail account, then certainly block his e-mail account. You may have to do this blocking again and again if he simply changes his e-mail to get through to you.

Legally, you are probably the victim of the crime of cyberstalking, which is a Class 2 misdemeanor. You should preserve the electronic e-mail file and also print a copy. Take the worst of the e-mails to the magistrate's office and ask to swear out a warrant under North Carolina General Statutes Section 14-196.3. This statute prohibits the use of any electronic communication that threatens or harasses or torments. E-mails, texts, and faxes are all electronic communications under this cyberstalking statute.

Another civil legal option is a Domestic Violence Protective Order. The Family Justice Center in Greensboro or High Point can help you with your complaint about a 50B for free. Print your e-mails and see one of the agents at the Family Justice Center. The pattern of harassment of the e-mails and the veiled threat to the dog's health and your health, in my opinion, qualify for relief under the Domestic Violence Protection laws under Chapter 50B of the North Carolina General Statutes. I agree with you that these comments about health were veiled threats designed to scare you.

I find it interesting that he broke up with you via e-mail. I don't know your age or how long you dated, but I don't like the growing etiquette problem of breaking up with electronic communication. I think of the divorce of Katy Perry from Russell Brand in 2011. Russell sent her a text message saying he was getting a divorce. Apparently, Russell used texting as a control strategy, and Katy publicly called out his controlling ways.

Katy Perry said: "Beautiful mind, tortured soul; I do have to figure out why I am attracted to these broken birds."

One final practical thing you can do is seek some counseling to see if you need to hone your skills of staying away from controlling men. Learn to spot this unsavory characteristic. Good luck with your next relationship.

## CONFRONTING SEXUAL ABUSE

Dear Carolyn:

I am now 32, and my sister is 35. We were both molested by our stepfather. Our mother "knew," but for whatever reason, selected to ignore this. My stepfather is now deceased, and he took his ugly secret to his grave. This stepfather has other children, all older than my sister and me. I would like closure regarding this horrific secret. I am thinking I would like to confront my mother about allowing this to happen and expose the b ..... d to his other children. What do I do?

*Molested*

Carolyn Answers ...

Dear Molested,

What a tragic story of domestic violence and criminal activity! The first role of a parent is to provide safety for the child, and neither your mother nor the stepfather offered protection.

Your first concern should be for yourself and your mental health. You need counseling by a counselor skilled in dealing with victims of child molestation. Perhaps you and your sister could do some joint counseling since you share this issue. You can provide comfort to each other and healing for each other.

Your mother for some reason could not provide safety. While there may be many reasons, a common one is that she is part of a "cycle of abuse," and in other words, she may have been a victim of molestation herself. She may have a crack in her "reality" that prevents her from dealing with molestation. Discuss with the counselor how you can make sure that you do not continue the "cycle of abuse." Depending on what your therapist says, you may, at some point, include your mother in counseling, but don't be surprised if she remains in denial.

Should you tell the children of your stepfather? Again, this is a topic for your counselor. If you tell them, be prepared for them to call you a liar as that is the most likely result of the disclosure to them. They probably are not going to believe you.

A word about pedophilia: Pedophilia is a psychiatric disorder first recognized in the nineteenth century, but one that has probably existed since the beginning of the human race. Pedophilia is the sexual attraction to prepubescent children. Pedophiles frequently are rabid consumers of child pornography. Detecting the use of child porn should be a big red flag. Most dangerous is the subpart of pedophilia known as infant philia, where the pedophile is sexually attracted to children ages 0 to 3 (but perhaps as old as 5). These children have little chance of reporting because of their tender age. If they do report, they are ignored as unreliable.

Parents, it is highly important for you to do know everything about anyone caring for your children.

Good luck on your recovery!

## EXPIRING PROTECTIVE ORDER

Dear Carolyn:

I have a domestic violence protective order, but the 1 year expires next month. I am still afraid of her. She came at me with a knife, but luckily, I was able to get away. She still posts statements on Facebook that let me know she is still angry with me. What do I do for protection when the 1 year is up?

*Need Protection*

Carolyn Answers ...

Dear Need Protection,

You can apply to the court to extend your domestic violence protective (DVPO) order for another year. Go to the clerk of court's office and the clerk will have a person who can help you with the paperwork (motion) you need to file. You can also contact the new Family Justice Center here in Guilford County by calling (336) 641-SAFE (7233). They will help you with the paperwork.

Interestingly, under North Carolina General Statutes Section 50B-3 and case law, there is nothing that prevents the judge from renewing a DVPO, based upon what happened in the past that allowed you to obtain the DVPO initially. You are going to need to re-explain what happened when she came at you with the knife. In Guilford County, you will likely not have the same judge you did a year ago.

Two other factors are important to your case: 1) you are still afraid, and 2) the Facebook posts showing that the anger of your ex has not subsided significantly. You do not say how you obtained the Facebook posts, as I assume you are not "friends" with your ex on Facebook. For the hearing, you may want to take with you the person who obtained the Facebook posts for you.

The Raleigh case of *Forehand v. Forehand* helps your situation. In *Forehand*, the plaintiff, who wanted to extend her DVPO, stated that she was "fearful of being put in the same room with the defendant without a DVPO in place." She further stated that if the DVPO were lifted, "he would be at my doorstep tonight. And I fear for the safety ... harm to the children, what he might do in their presence ..." The defendant didn't think that was enough for an extension, so he appealed to the North Carolina Court of Appeals and lost.

I particularly like the *Forehand* case because it clearly talks about the subjective fear of the plaintiff as the important factor. Lawyers like to debate objective fear vs. subjective fear. Generally, subjective fear is your personal fear, regardless of whether others would be afraid under similar circumstances. Objective fear asks the question: "Would the reasonable person be fearful under the circumstances?" The standard for a DVPO is subjective fear as stated in *Forehand*.

Please write down all of the facts that give you cause for concern and make you want to obtain an extension of your DVPO. Many of these cases are lost because of failure to "make your case." The judge has to hear all facts. Be sure to take the Facebook posts you mentioned with you, and perhaps, the person who obtained the Facebook posts for you.

## GUN POSSESSION IN DOMESTIC VIOLENCE CASES

Dear Carolyn:

I want my guns back. My ex-wife filed a 50B for domestic violence that never happened, and the judge took my guns away. The incident, she fabricated, didn't even involve a gun. The year is up, so how do I get my guns back?

*It's My Gun*

Carolyn Answers ...

Dear It's My Gun,

Unless the court extends the Domestic Violence Protective Order (DVPO) for your ex after the year is up, you are likely entitled to get your guns back. The sheriff of Guilford County is holding your guns (assuming you are from Guilford). You must file a motion to the court and request a time for a hearing. You need to do this quickly after the year is up; do not wait. You only have 90 days.

At the hearing, the court must determine whether there are any other laws that prevent you from owning or possessing firearms. For example, if you are a felon or if you are on probation that precludes firearms, you will not get your guns back from the judge. Otherwise, your guns will likely be returned with an order of the district court granting you the right to the return of your guns from the sheriff.

One factor that bothers me about your fact pattern is that the court must make certain findings to remove guns from a defendant when the court grants a DVPO. Nothing you mention in your question suggests that the judge should have removed your guns. I think this is a misunderstood point under the domestic violence law. Just because the court grants a DVPO doesn't automatically mean that the court can remove a defendant's firearms. Let's look at when the judge can remove firearms in granting a DVPO.

North Carolina General Statutes Section 50B-3.1(a) enumerates four situations or factors. The judge specifically must find one of the four factors to order the defendant to surrender firearms to the sheriff. These factors are as follows:

1. The use or threatened use of a deadly weapon by the defendant or a pattern of prior conduct involving the use or threatened use of violence with a firearm against persons.
2. Threats to seriously injure or kill the aggrieved party or minor child by the defendant.
3. Threats to commit suicide by the defendant.
4. Serious injuries inflicted upon the aggrieved party or minor child by the defendant.

In the recent case of *Griffin v. Reichard*, the North Carolina Court of Appeals reversed a New Hanover County District Court judge for ordering the surrender of firearms in a DVPO without the findings of one of the specific four factors. The Court of Appeals discussed in detail that removal of a defendant's firearms cannot be part of the general relief of granting a DVPO, but must have more findings specifically related to the firearms.

Dear Carolyn:

I read your column on July 9 concerning guns and 50Bs—the one where the guy wanted his guns back after the year of the 50B was up. You told him to file a motion within 90 days. My question is: what happens to the guns collected in 50Bs when the motion for return of the gun is not filed?

*Gun Owner*

Carolyn Answers ...

Dear Gun Owner,

The sheriff asks the court for a disposition order for the gun. The court has several options for the disposition of the guns collected by the sheriff in a 50B and unclaimed after the 50B expires pursuant to North Carolina General Statutes Section 14-269.1. At the court's direction,

1. The sheriff will destroy the gun if there is no serial number;
2. The sheriff will destroy the gun if the gun is unsafe;
3. The sheriff will turn over to N.C. State Crime Lab for the gun to be in the weapon reference library; or
4. The sheriff will turn over the weapon to the N.C. Justice Academy.

## PRESENTING DRUG PARAPHERNALIA AS EVIDENCE

Dear Carolyn:

I read the article Mr. Yost wrote on May 28, 2015, in *Rhino* concerning the man who took marijuana to the courtroom in Greensboro. My ex-spouse smokes marijuana, and we are getting ready for a custody trial over our 3-year-old. After my ex moved out, I found some drug paraphernalia the ex left behind in my home. I found a ceramic pipe, and I know what my ex used this for. I have never used drugs, and this is one of the reasons we broke up. I want to use this as evidence in my custody trial, but now I am afraid to take the evidence to the court to show the judge. What should I do? The judge needs to see the evidence I have. I do not have an attorney, at least not yet. I don't want to end up like Mr. Hussain, in jail.

*Concerned*

Carolyn Answers ...

Dear Concerned,

Your concern is fairly common in custody cases, and there are a lot of custody cases where one spouse has evidence of the other spouse's illegal drug use. So how do you present this evidence?

First, you need to recognize that North Carolina General Statutes Section 90-113.20 makes it illegal to possess drug paraphernalia, and the statutes detail many different items considered drug paraphernalia. A ceramic pipe is listed in the definition of drug paraphernalia. The statute further states that the intent of the owner or the possessor of the pipe is to use the pipe to violate the Controlled Substances Act. From what you say, your intent is not to use the pipe for violation of the Controlled Substances Act, but I would still use caution. You cannot march into the courtroom with this pipe; that is a bad idea.

Your evidence is going to be good quality photographs of what you found. It is that simple. I recommend that you take a picture showing the item in the place where you found it, presumably hidden. If you have moved the pipe, you will move it back to its original hiding place, but you will have to disclose that you had already moved it.

Now, what do you do with the pipe itself? This is a more difficult question, and I suggest you hire an attorney. You really have two choices: destroy the pipe or give it to the police. I never favor the destruction of evidence. Thus, you need to get the pipe to the police and have them take control of the pipe. Under no circumstances should the police be called to your home, as you are in possession of an item that is obviously problematic. Your attorney also is not going to want to be in the chain of custody of the pipe. But, your attorney will probably know a law enforcement officer who will meet you at the lawyer's office or other location and take possession of the pipe. The police officer should make a police report. Then you have the ability to subpoena the officer to court giving you corroboration that the pipe existed.

# CHAPTER 8

## Property Division

### GENERAL OVERVIEW

The court (unless settled by agreement any time after separation) will divide the property owned by you and your spouse. You MUST have a claim for equitable distribution pending on the date of the absolute divorce or your rights are gone. In North Carolina, this process is described as "Equitable Distribution of Marital Assets."

There are three types of property that must be considered.

   a. "Separate property" includes all property owned by either spouse before the marriage or property acquired during the marriage by one spouse by inheritance or gift from a third party. A gift from one spouse to the other during the marriage is marital property unless the donor states at the time of the conveyance that it is intended to be separate property.
   b. "Marital Property" includes property presently owned that was acquired during the marriage except property determined to be "separate property." "Marital property" includes all vested pension and retirement benefits acquired during the marriage and prior to separation.
   c. "Divisible property" is relatively new. Divisible property is property subject to equitable distribution upon divorce and is defined as real

and personal property that includes the appreciation and diminution in value of marital property and other divisible property acquired as a result of actions of the parties during the marriage but before separation, passive income from marital property received after separation, and increases in marital debt including finance charges and interest related to marital debt.

The law further creates a presumption that an in-kind distribution of marital or divisible property is equitable, but allows this presumption to be rebutted by the greater weight of the evidence or by evidence that the property is a closely held business entity or is otherwise not susceptible of division in-kind.

## PROTECTING BUSINESS DURING SEPARATION

Dear Carolyn:

We have a small family business. I do all the work with customers; my ex does the bookkeeping. My wife does the bookkeeping. We both own the company as shareholders. We now are now separated. What protections do I need to put in place? She writes checks that are not for business expenses out of the business account.

*Concerned*

Carolyn Answers ...

Dear Concerned,

It is rare for a couple to be able to continue in a small business together after divorce. There is just too much friction. I will give you some general tips, but go over your situation with a family lawyer of your choice. First, take care of your customers and keep them out of the divorce drama as much as possible. Do not use your customers as confidants. Second, consider hiring an independent bookkeeper. I strongly recommend that you review invoices and sign the checks yourself. You also may need to change signature cards at the bank. Third, if your ex needs money from the company, consider a draw for her for her personal use. You may want to establish a draw for yourself as well. Fourth, you need to document exactly where the business is that the date of separation. You need an interim financial statement at the date of separation. For example, you need to document the balances of loans, financial account balances, receivables balances, and inventories at the date of separation. The date of separation is the date of valuation for equitable distribution, which is the property division statute. Finally, if reason does not prevail, a motion for a restraining order might help maintain a feasible situation for you and your customers.

## EX-SPOUSE HIDING ASSETS

Dear Carolyn:

I am afraid my doctor husband is hiding assets. I'm pretty sure he plans to divorce me. He has a passport, and he leaves town sometimes, and I don't know where he goes. I sneaked and looked at his passport and see entries to Panama and the Cayman Islands. He likes to fish, but I do not feel these are fishing trips. How do I make sure he doesn't hide the assets so I cannot find them in our divorce if that happens? I don't know much about our assets. My husband works for one of the big Greensboro medical practices.

*Afraid*

Carolyn Answers ...

Dear Afraid,

There are many, many things you can do to make sure you get half (or more) of the assets of the marriage in your property division. No asset can really be hidden if you are willing to put the time and money into finding the asset(s).

Tracing is the key. In your particular case, tracing will start with the tax returns and the income your husband receives from his medical practice. Your attorney and forensic accountant will trace the income from the medical practice forward looking at all aspects of how the money was used. Tracing today involves tracing how funds are transferred electronically. You will need to use in your divorce the process of "discovery," which allows your attorney to mandate that your husband and third-party recordkeepers (banks, credit unions, etc.) give records for analysis to your lawyer.

But, what if the money seems to disappear mysteriously? Poof, into thin air! You mention passport entries out of the U.S., so let's discuss offshore accounts for hiding assets. There is a recent, high-profile case you need to consider. Dr. Michael Brandner, a plastic surgeon, was married for 28 years. Brandner's wife filed for divorce. He took $3 million and converted it into cashier's checks, and then off to Costa Rica he went. Once in Costa Rica, he deposited some of the cashier's checks and then put a thousand ounces of gold in a safety deposit box. He then traveled to Panama where he created a shell corporation called "Dakota Investment" and deposited money into this sham company.

Brandner got his just desserts and was prosecuted, primarily because he did not report the accounts on his tax returns. He seems not to have intended to cheat the IRS, but rather to cheat his wife. During his divorce, he claimed the money was tied up in these investments and could not be returned because the investments were lost. Oops! But, Brandner is serving 48 months for wire fraud and tax evasion.

So after Dr. Brandner is out of federal prison, how does Mrs. Brandner recover her half if Dr. Brandner is still being a bad boy? The family court judge will have to require Dr. Brandner to allow the assets to be released to Ms. Brandner and can jail him for contempt until he does so. These are difficult cases, but you also may have to file ancillary lawsuits in the foreign countries to gain access to the accounts. It will also be helpful for you to understand the 2010 federal law that allows the U.S. to freeze foreign accounts under certain circumstances.

In addition to all of the above, please look out for expensive collectibles, such as valuable paintings, which could be hiding value right before your very eyes.

## ESTATE PLANNING AND IN-LAWS

### Dear Carolyn:

My wife and I are age 60. We are doing *estate planning*. We own a commercial real estate building that is quite valuable. The building is in an LLC. I want to transfer this to my son at a price below fair market value in the estate planning process; I want my son to have this commercial property. My concern is that my son and his wife (both age 40) may not have a stable marriage. My wife and I would like to make this a joint gift from the two of us to the two of them for gift tax purposes, but what happens to the real estate if we make this bargain transfer to the two of them, and then they divorce? Do you have any advice or insight?

*Charitable, but Want to Be Wise*

Carolyn Answers ...

Dear Charitable:

This is a common estate and gift planning problem and needs to be handled with great care. I have been faced with this scenario after the fact on many occasions, and you need to both understand the law AND make sure the documents reflect your intent very clearly.

One recent case that you need to understand is *Montague v. Montague, Harvey Lynwood Montague Jr. v. Teresa Montague*. In that case, the husband's parents gave the couple a commercial building in an LLC (which is a common form of ownership of commercial property in North Carolina) that the husband subsequently managed. Luckily, the trial judge recognized the bargain purchase nature of the gift and recognized Mr. Montague's parents' estate planning intent. Smart trial judge in Wake County. It was undisputed in *Montague* that neither party to the divorce proceeding made "equity" contributions to the LLC. The trial court, however, treated the property as marital property but gave husband an unequal division because of his parents' transfer of the LLC to the now divorcing couple. The wife appealed to the North Carolina Court of Appeals wanting her "half" of the LLC. Luckily, the trial judge in Wake County made lots of findings of fact, and the wife lost.

So, from a planning point of view, please do not rely on what might happen in litigation or what happened in *Montague*. It might not happen in your case if your son and his wife get a divorce. Here's what I would do if I wanted to ensure the result. I would require the couple (your son and his wife) to execute a post-martial agreement concerning what happens to the LLC in the event of a divorce of your son and his wife. You may also want to consider what your intent is with regard to where the property goes if your son predeceases your daughter-in-law. After all, this is your gift, and you can do what you please with your property.

Your son's wife will have to have an attorney go over the document with her or the document may not hold up; this is very important. You son will need an attorney to go over it with him, as well. Your son and his wife should not use the same attorney. If they will not do the postmarital agreement, you need to look at other options for the transfer of the property that achieves your intended result. There may be a trust option available.

While all of this seems harsh, reality is reality and divorce is common. Planning is important.

## QUALIFIED DOMESTIC RELATIONS ORDER

Dear Carolyn:

I have a 401(k) at work, and I am going through a divorce. I understand there are lots of penalties if I give my ex half. This is really the major asset left to be divided as we sold our home and divided the proceeds. I do not have the cash to buy her out of my 401(k). What are my options?

*Not Interested in the Tax Penalties*

Carolyn Answers ...

Dear Not Interested,

If the 401(k) was acquired totally during the marriage, then it is marital property to be divided presumptively 50-50. The 401(k) can be divided "in kind" with a Qualified Domestic Relations Order (commonly referred to as a "QDRO," generally pronounced "quad-row" or "Q-drow"). There is no penalty associated with a properly drafted and qualified QDRO. Generally, the 401(k) is divided in half, and your ex's half is rolled into an IRA for the ex. It sounds like you are going to have to use a QDRO since you do not have the cash to buy the ex out.

## COLLEGE FUNDS IN EQUITABLE DISTRIBUTION

Dear Carolyn:

I am in the middle of an equitable distribution divorce case. A year ago, we started contributing to a college fund for our son under what is called a UTMA account. What is a UTMA account? Also, since it is in our son's name, how is this considered in my property settlement? My husband says that it is marital property, and he wants his half.

*Unsure*

Carolyn Answers ...

Dear Unsure,

You are asking about a hot topic in divorce settlements in North Carolina right now. I'll first describe and define UTMA. Then, I'll discuss the recent hot issue.

UTMA means Uniform Transfers to Minors Act, which is legislatively defined under North Carolina General Statutes Section 33A. The word "uniform" is used when a state adopts legislation that has also been adopted in most other states to enhance mobility between states. A donor transfers the gift property to a custodian until the minor reaches age 21. I sometimes see bank statements where money is transferred to a bank account that is designated as a UTMA account. At age 14, the minor has the right to demand inspection of the records of the property held by the custodian, but I have never seen a 14-year-old do this unless prompted by the other parent (perhaps in a divorce situation). The custodian may distribute money to support the minor, but mostly these funds are intended for college.

The Court of Appeals in Raleigh on January 19, 2016, rendered an opinion on a Wells Fargo UTMA account. *Carpenter v. Carpenter*. The plaintiff mother apparently alleged that $188,648.52 in a UTMA account held for the minor son be distributed to the defendant father who was the custodial parent of the minor son and charged against him as marital property. There were technical problems with the appeal, but the Court of Appeals did comment: "When a third party holds legal title to property which is claimed to be marital property, that third party is a necessary party to the equitable distribution proceeding with their participation limited to the issue of the ownership of that property." I cannot imagine that equitable distribution courts will (or should) take the college money of minors in UTMA accounts and distribute these funds as marital property.

Marital property under the equitable distribution statute should be property owned at the date of separation. The ownership of the *Carpenter* UTMA was with the third party, known as the custodian. Unless the father had dumped money in the UTMA on the eve of the date of separation, this UTMA account rightly belonged to the minor son and not the marital estate.

# CHAPTER 9

# Technology and Social Media

## ▦ GENERAL OVERVIEW

Technology and how it affects families is rapidly changing. Eight-year-olds have cell phones and iPads. Managing Twitter, Facebook, and the media flavor of the day adds new challenges to parenting, particularly parenting children of divorce. The Internet has many dangers for children. How do we protect them from violence and predators? What do you do when Mom's philosophy and Dad's philosophy differ?

How does one collect evidence of an illicit sexual relationship with Snapchat? Text messaging seems to be the main communication method for many persons divorcing; yet, we cannot recover the texts from Verizon or other vendors, only from the cell phone itself. Are we headed for a world where evidence simply disappears into the cloud like Hillary Clinton's e-mails?

## ▦ FACETIME VISITATION

Dear Carolyn:

My child's mother lives in Raleigh. The mother visits every other weekend with the child, but we are going to court soon, and the mother wants to use FaceTime with the child. I think this will be a pain in the b----, but what do you think the court might say about using FaceTime for visitation? I don't have an iPad, and neither does the child. I do have one FaceTime with the mother's new boyfriend scantly clad in the background.

*Concerned about FaceTime*

Carolyn Answers ...

Dear Concerned,

Welcome to the world of custody in 2016. For my readers, FaceTime is a videotelephony application that basically allows two or more people to talk remotely and see each other at the same time. This has become such the "deal" in remote parent-child visitation that the legislature in Raleigh has added provisions to NCGS 50-13.2(e) concerning "electronic visitation" with a child.

Here are the issues the court will review with you:

1. Is the video visitation in the child's best interest?
2. Is the video equipment accessible, affordable, and available in both parents' homes? In your case, you don't have an iPad, which is needed for FaceTime. However, you may have an Android device or a computer that will play programs similar to FaceTime. This might be Skype, Viber, or Google Hangouts. You might research these alternative programs to see if anything works on a device you have.
3. The court can consider any other factor the court deems appropriate. Well, this might be where you talk about the absence of clothing on the boyfriend during FaceTime with a child.
4. The court can set guidelines for the video visitation, such as the hours and length of time for video visitation. I suggest you have a plan of what you would like to present to the court when you go. For example, you might tell the judge that you would like the video visitation on Thursday nights at 7 p.m. The length of the video chat depends on the age of the child. I do not know how old your child is.
5. The court can implement a cost-sharing for the equipment for video visitation. This is not a part of child support and is a separate custody item.

6. Video visitation can supplement physical visitation, but cannot replace it entirely.
7. The electronic visitation can be supervised if ordered by the court.
8. Electronic visitation is not a factor in child support.

Oh, and you might send the boyfriend a shirt and pants to wear. Sounds like he needs clothes. LOL.

## GPS TRACKING

Dear Carolyn:

Can I put an electronic tracking device (GPS) on my ex's car? My private investigator doesn't want to do it and says there is a new law on this. I think my ex is doing drug deals, and I want to track him for evidence in my child custody case that is coming up in April. Can you help me understand what to do?

GPS

Carolyn Answers ...

Dear GPS,

There is a brand-new law effective December 1, 2015, that makes attaching a GPS to someone's car the crime of cyberstalking, except under specific circumstances. Cyberstalking is a Class 2 misdemeanor, which could mean any sentence between community service to 60 days in jail. NCGS Section 14-196.3.

Most of the special circumstances are for law enforcement, but there are several that apply in divorce and family law matters.

**Exception 1:** If you are a parent or legal guardian of a minor child, you can track the minor child. The law is vague on whether the vehicle must be driven by the minor, or whether the minor can simply be a passenger. The law is also vague on whether a parent with joint legal custody can track the other joint legal custodian when the minor child is a passenger. The law is quite clear that the tracking device cannot be on the "person" of the caretaker of your child.

**Exception 2:** This exception allows a licensed private investigator in the normal course of his/her business to place a GPS tracking device on a vehicle with the consent of the owner of the vehicle. "Owner" is not defined, and I hear the argument all the time that a vehicle owned before separation and subject to equitable distribution is jointly owned if it is marital property. I would not advise a client to place a GPS device on a vehicle under the "marital property" theory of ownership. I think it is unlikely that "owner" would be defined as equitable ownership. The owner would logically include the person or entity that holds the "title" as registered with the Department of Motor Vehicles.

**Exception 3:** Hurrah for domestic violence with another helpful law. Let's look at this scenario to understand the 50B (domestic violence protective order) provision. Let's say wife receives a 50B domestic violence protective order. The 50B provides wife has possession of the family vehicle titled to husband. Husband believes his wife is having an illicit sexual relationship. Husband would like to track her. His name is on the title to the vehicle. The new law precludes and prohibits the perpetrator husband and his private investigator from placing a tracking device on a vehicle, even though it is titled to husband. I think there is a risk here for private detectives, because what if the husband doesn't tell the detective about the 50B? What if a husband only shows the detective the title to the vehicle? Lucky for the detective community, the detective must "knowingly" violate the statute, which is the case for most criminal statutes.

## SPYWARE

Dear Carolyn:

I am a mother with primary custody of a 9-year-old daughter. The father has visitation. For Christmas, he bought our daughter a smartphone, but he did not discuss this with me. He had spyware on the smartphone that allowed him to see her opening the Christmas present. I thought that he disengaged the spyware after she opened the present, but I just found out that the spyware is still engaged on my daughter's phone. This smartphone allows him to track everywhere we go. He told our daughter to be sure to keep the phone with her, particularly when she is with Mommy. His spying makes me feel eerie. We are divorced, so why does he want to know where I am? What should I do?

*Eerie*

Carolyn Answers ...

> Dear Eerie,
>
> Your questions raise many interesting issues: What age should a child receive a smartphone? What do you do about mobile tracking and spyware? What do you do about controlling behavior after the relationship is over?
>
> The age a child should receive a smartphone is child specific. A child's first phone should not be a smartphone, but merely a cell phone that allows the child to call 911 and home, but the parent should block other uses of the phone. That might be appropriate for a 9-year-old. I would not allow a 9-year-old to have a smartphone, at least not unsupervised. As the child progresses into a smartphone, the parent should block all access to pornography and other inappropriate sites. I would also block access to violence. Parents also have to decide how much texting is healthy for their child. There are several phones designed especially for children. You might look at www.mashable.com for "7 Best Cellphones for Kids."
>
> It is unclear in your question if you are calling the "location" service of a smartphone spyware, or if there is a particular additional spyware program on the smartphone. You can turn off the "location" service under "settings." Spyware is another issue. You may want to engage a digital forensic examiner to review the phone and preserve evidence, particularly if you think a crime may have been committed.
>
> I am concerned that your ex told your daughter to have the phone when with Mommy. It appears you ex wants to know where you are. Why does he want to know? That is controlling behavior in the best case. You should be alert to any other controlling or harassing behavior because this conduct could be a red flag. For example, does he drive through your neighborhood? Stalking is both criminal and domestic violence. Keep your eyes open.

Dear Carolyn:

> I was angry at that father who bought the child the smartphone to monitor "Mommy" in your July 9 column. What can the mother do to stop this? Can she get custody?

*No More Spying*

Carolyn Answers ...

> Dear No More Spying,
> I believe that the mother from the July 9 question had primary custody, so the real question probably is: What can be done against spying if there is already a custody order and the spy is spying on the parent with primary custody? This answer will not include opportunities for criminal prosecution, if any, which can be discussed with the magistrate.
> There are two legal possibilities, other than the practical one of simply removing the phone from the child and substituting a child-safe telephone. First, a victim might try for a domestic violence protective under the concept of a continuing harassment. I think you will get varying results from judges. Second, you could ask for a custody modification or a restraining order in the child custody action. Neither of the legal options are as attractive to me as simply removing the smartphone from the young child.
> In *Hassell v. Hassell*, the North Carolina Court of Appeals recently affirmed primary custody for a mother where the father had given an 8-year-old a smartphone loaded with spyware. The court considered the bad behavior of spying in awarding the father less time with the child.

Carolyn Blogs On ...

## ■■ CAUGHT BY THE IPAD!

One of my favorite stars is Gwen Stefani. She manages a life of motherhood, career with celebrity status, and fashion. And, now, she has just completed a divorce with her 13-year marriage to Gavin Rossdale, which produced Apollo (almost 2), Kingston (age 9), and Zuma (age 7). Rumors swirl that Gavin had an affair with the nanny, and Gwen apparently found nude photos of the nanny and plans for Gavin and the nanny to meet for sex—**all found on the family iPad. The information on the family iPad yielded an abrupt end to this marriage.** Gavin had naughty behavior that uploaded from his iPhone to the cloud and downloaded to the linked family iPad.

**Yes, this unintentional spying could happen in the North Carolina divorce. Why? The iCloud (or any cloud), iPad, iPhone, and other electronic devices are everywhere, and they link to each other.** While perhaps we all know this, we are trusting, I believe, or maybe simply not observant. There is the substantial risk that the children could see the naughty electronic evidence.

How could this iPad information be used in your case in Greensboro? There are three major times your now ex-spouse might be looking for "dirty" information on you: 1) custody; 2) divorce from bed and board; and 3) spousal support or alimony. For a bonus, if Gwen had been in North Carolina, she could have used the iPad in an alienation of affection and criminal conversation case against the nanny.

How do you preserve the iPad evidence? Can't it be just erased from the iPad by deleting it from the iPhone and the iCloud? Yes, this naughty evidence can be deleted. Deleting evidence can be spoliation of evidence, and spoliation can be severely held against you in court. If you do elect to eliminate the iPad evidence, you need to preserve a copy somewhere should you need it.

If you are the non-naughty spouse, you want to preserve the iPad. Your first step is to disconnect the iPad from the iCloud or another cloud so that the information cannot be remotely deleted. Then, if you can, cease using the iPad with the evidence and preserve it in a secure location away from your home.

You cannot just cut and paste the jpegs or other files to a new file on your computer as you are possibly interrupting the chain of custody. You could hire a digital forensic expert to copy exactly the items on the computer and maintain the chain of custody, but this is expensive.

Gwen and Gavin settled their marital estate in October 2015, and during that same month, she released the new single "Used to Love You." Her life blew up in her face in February, the day after the Grammy's, and she used her music to work through the earthquake emotions of divorce. *"I don't know why I cry/But I think it's cause I remembered for the first time/Since I hated you/That I used to love you,"* rings Gwen's gut-wrenching song.

By the way, she got the house in Beverly Hills, and her attitude is positive energy.

# CHAPTER 10

# Miscellaneous

## COLLABORATIVE LAW

Dear Carolyn:

I hear a term used "collaborative law." I am thinking of getting a divorce, and I am looking at options. What is "collaborative law"? What are the pros and the cons?

*Researching*

Carolyn Answers ...

Dear Researching,

There are several different approaches to finding a resolution to divorce cases, such as mediation, arbitration, court, and collaborative law. North Carolina has statutes that define collaborative law in North Carolina General Statutes Section 50-70 et seq.

What is collaborative law? Collaborative law is defined in North Carolina General Statutes 50-71. A married couple is contemplating divorce, and their respective attorneys agree to use best efforts to settle the matrimonial issues outside the courtroom. Procedurally, the married couple agrees to attempt to settle out of court. If litigation subsequently goes forward in the court, then the attorneys in the collaborative process cannot serve as litigation counsel. A collaborative law agreement must be in writing and signed by both parties before a notary. The agreement must have the withdrawal provisions for both attorneys if the collaborative process fails. A collaborative agreement can provide that the lawyers for the collaborative process can continue with the use of arbitration or other alternate dispute resolution. The collaborative agreement cannot provide that the lawyers will continue if contested litigation is involved.

Collaborative law agreements frequently have the parties using the same expert to get to an answer on difficult issues in the marital dissolution, such as business valuation and child custody. A couple participating in collaborative law might jointly hire a business appraiser to place a value on the marital business with the idea that the joint appraiser's value will be used to resolve that issue in the case. The couple might jointly employ a licensed psychologist with credentials as a child custody evaluator to help them decide custodial issues with the children.

Who should use collaborative law? My opinion is that persons should use collaborative law only if they have relatively equal knowledge of the facts and relative equal bargaining power and strengths. The divorce also needs to be very friendly. Frequently, the party with control of the information wants to use collaborative law, and then will not timely give over complete and adequate information for the process to go forward.

Some of the negatives requiring careful consideration are as follows:

1. The loss of counsel is a big issue because both parties have to start all over with new lawyers if litigation is needed. It can be expensive to start over.
2. You lose the work done by the third-party experts. All statements, communications in the collaborative are inadmissible in any court proceeding; this work is privileged and inadmissible. A business valuation costs several thousand dollars, and this is lost, unless the parties agree that a third-party expert's work is admissible.
3. I frequently scratch my head and say, isn't collaborative law good old-fashioned lawyering and negotiating? Lawyers have negotiated since lawyers were created. Why pay for an agreement to reach another agreement?

Carolyn Blogs On ...

## CRITICAL ISSUES FOR SAME-SEX MARRIAGE

1. What is the date of marriage? Prior to October 2014, same-sex couples could not marry in North Carolina. But what date of marriage will North Carolina recognize if the same-sex couple was earlier married or entered into a civil union in some other state before October 2014? The date of marriage is obviously critical in equitable distribution as marital property is created from the date of marriage to the date of separation. The North Carolina legislature has not dealt with this important date of marriage issue (civil union date) where the couple married (created a civil union) in another state prior to October 2014.

   *a.* Arguably, the date of marriage is the date of the marriage license and ceremony in a state that recognized same-sex marriage on the actual date of the marriage. North Carolina should recognize that original marriage date because the couple could return to the state of the marriage and get a divorce.

   *b.* What about the civil union? Some states now have an opt-in provision turning the civil union into a marriage. So will the date of the marriage be the date of the civil union or the date of the opt-in to marriage? North Carolina does not have an opt-in provision.

   *c.* In Vermont, a civil union statute automatically turns the civil union into a marriage by a Vermont statute. In 2012, the Massachusetts Supreme Court declared that a Vermont civil union is equivalent to marriage. *Elia-Warnken v. Elia*, 163 Mass. 29 (2012).

   *d.* Civil unions were created primarily as a workaround for marriage. People entered civil unions to obtain rights of marriage. Is civil union marriage, or is it something else? North Carolina never had a civil union statute, but what if a couple has a civil union in a state with an opt-in provision for marriage and they did not opt in. Will North Carolina consider them married if there was no opt-in to marriage? The member of the civil union that does not want a marriage will argue: I have no notice that I am married; I would have had a premarital agreement if I was getting married.

e. Should intent of the couple in entering the civil union be part of the decision in North Carolina on whether the civil union is recognized as a marriage? The intent analysis seems messy and open-ended to me, as intents (reasons) vary widely and have many individual ramifications. Should there be a rebuttable presumption that persons to a civil union intended to be married?

f. Let's say at the date of marriage in Canada, one of the partners to the same-sex partnership was married to someone else in North Carolina and were not divorced from spouse one. So is the marriage in Canada a marriage? Is it bigamy?

g. North Carolina will not likely recognize civil unions as marriage.

h. North Carolina has many issues to resolve either through the legislature or the courts regarding marriages and civil unions in other states or countries if the marriage or civil union occurred before October 2014.

2. Gay and lesbian couples create families generally through surrogates or adoption. North Carolina does not recognize the Uniform Parentage Act.

a. *Joint Adoption.* In North Carolina, a married gay or lesbian couple may jointly adopt a child.

b. *Stepparent adoption.* If one member of the gay or lesbian couple is a biological parent and the other marriage partner is not biological, a stepparent adoption may be possible. North Carolina General Statutes Section 48-2-301(c). Note that the couple must have been married at least 6 months for a stepparent adoption. Then there is the question of whether you need a termination of parental rights if there was an anonymous sperm donor.

c. *Surrogate.* Both same-sex and opposite-sex couples have children with the use of a surrogate. North Carolina has a presumption that a child born during the marriage is the child of both parents. Logically, in a married gay or lesbian couple, one of the partners is not a biological parent, so should this presumption apply? For example, the married gay male couple may use a surrogate, so one is a biological parent and one is not.

The Department of Health and Human Services in North Carolina is currently unwilling to utilize this marital presumption to married gay men. So, currently, in North Carolina, the nonbiological parent will need to get a declaration of parentage. Otherwise, you may need to get a termination of parental rights of the surrogate.

## UN-NEIGHBORLY CONDUCT

Dear Carolyn:

My neighbors recently went on vacation and left their college-age son, who is home for the summer, without supervision in their home. The son gave an outrageous party, and I called the police. I think there was underage drinking. I think one child was hurt as I saw an ambulance. I am just curious about the conduct of my neighbors who own their home in our otherwise peaceful neighborhood.

*Concerned Neighbor*

Carolyn Answers ...

Dear Concerned Neighbor,

You should be concerned. According to much recent brain research, the typical brain in the United States is not mature until age 25 on the average. Judgment is impaired with immature decision making. Property owners, please beware that you can be liable for the actions of others on your property. To me, there is a moral reasonability, even if the *Leonard* case I describe hereafter makes civil liability doubtful.

In your question, the person giving the party is likely over 18 and thus, an adult. So the question of civil liability may turn on whether the adult property owners know what is going on.

The North Carolina Court of Appeals recently addressed the liability of parents who own a dwelling in *Leonard v. Transylvania DSS, Fisher, et al.* Barbara Leonard's 16-year-old son died after a party at the home owned by Shawn and Tracy Fisher. The Fisher's son, Scott, age 19, gave a party while his parents were out of town. Someone brought alcohol to the party. The Fishers did not know Scott would be throwing the party.

Michael Leonard, age 16, was injured in a fight at the Fisher residence. Michael was intoxicated. Michael left the party, and later that evening, he died of hypothermia after he apparently got out of a car in an isolated location away from the Fisher home. How Michael got to the isolated location is unclear, but he was probably too intoxicated to look after himself.

Scott Fisher was convicted of involuntary manslaughter but, in this instance, the *Leonard* case was before the Court of Appeals regarding the liability of Shawn and Tracy Fisher as the owners of the property to the estate of Michael Leonard. While the case is quite complicated, the Court of Appeals ruled that the property owners were not liable to the estate for money damages. The case seems to turn on the fact that Scott was 19 and the age of majority was 18; thus, the Fishers could not be presumed to control the adult son.

This was a nightmare for both the Fishers and the Leonards, so think twice before leaving persons under 25 in charge of your real property. The brain of the person under 26 may not be what you think. Neighbors should call the police in these party situations.

## UNGRATEFUL RELATIVES

Dear Carolyn:

I am an aunt with two adult nephews and one adult niece. I have no children of my own. I have been very faithful, I feel, to lavishing these ingrates with gifts and attention on holidays, at weddings, birthdays, baby showers, and generally. There is never a thank-you note from them, much less a gift (not even a small one). They virtually ignore me unless they are getting something from me. I am very careful to thank them for every little thing they do for me, but when I thank them, I get the rude comment of "no problem." Where did the manners go for "thank you" and "you're welcome"? Thanksgiving and Christmas are particularly hard when they are most of my "blood" family. I am considering simply washing my hands of these unappreciative relatives as I feel that would make me feel the best. Any advice?

*Tired of the Unthankful*

Carolyn Answers ...

Dear Tired of the Unthankful,

There are two aspects to your problem: (1) differences in generations and how they use language to express themselves; and (2) practical solutions that might make you feel better about your particular situation.

First, the generational issues are apparent from your facts. My guess from your facts as you presented them is that you are a baby boomer (born between 1946 and 1964). Further, my guess is that your niece and nephews are millennials (birth years from the early 1980s to early 2000s). Millennials and baby boomers do not usually agree on how to express thankfulness. Millennials will respond to a "thank you" with "no problem." A millennial would use "you're welcome" in a sarcastic tone to point out that a person for whom they did a favor did not thank them. Believe me, the millennials want to be thanked for any favor they perform. Other "minimizing" words used by millennials in response to "thank you" might be "no worries."

But, why are these millennials not thanking you for your generous gifts? Society is changing a bit perceived etiquette rules. In a *Vanity Fair* poll, only 23 percent of those surveyed considered thank-you notes important. Keep in mind millennials think breaking up with a significant other can be done with a text message.

Millennial Lizzie Post, the great-great-granddaughter of Emily Post, is now a coauthor of *Emily Post's Etiquette* (18th Edition). Thank-you notes are still "Post" etiquette if a gift is opened outside the presence of the giver, according to Lizzie. I suggest your next gift to your niece and nephews be a copy of *Emily Post's Etiquette* bookmarked to the thank-you note section. Include in the gift a box of thank-you notes, also. Make this the final gift until you get a handwritten note of appreciation for this gift.

## ADULT CHILDREN AND SUBSTANCE ABUSE

Dear Carolyn:

I am a concerned mother of a 19-year-old boy, who has a drug issue and is prone to suicidal threats. He did try to kill himself once when he was age 16, and he was placed in the behavioral health section of a local hospital for treatment. He has recently moved out of my home and into the home of some of his friends. What kind of legal options do I have?

*Need to Know*

**Carolyn Answers ...**

Dear Need to know,

You have a difficult situation and given that your son is legally an adult at 19 gives you very few legal options. There is one legal option of involuntary commitment, which I will discuss in paragraph two. But, first, practical advice. You have to practice tough love and not enable the boy's drug habit. You cannot "helicopter" in to save him at every turn. You obviously should not provide resources for purchasing drugs. Secure any weapons and ammunition you have so that he doesn't have access. Sometimes, you simply have to step back and pray.

The only real legal option is the option of involuntary commitment if he is a danger to himself or others. Persons who are suicidal can also be homicidal, so please keep that in mind. If you can keep track of your son without enabling him, you may be able to keep tabs on his mental health. Under the laws of North Carolina, you can go to the magistrate's office and file for involuntary commitment swearing to facts that your son is a danger to himself or others. The police will then pick up your son and take him to a mental health facility for evaluation. If the mental health professional agrees that he is a danger to himself or others, the professional will have your son hospitalized for mental health treatment. He will be entitled to a hearing within 10 days to determine whether further hospitalization is needed, and the court will appoint a lawyer for him.

Mental health and violence have become such a huge societal problem, so your facts can never be taken lightly. Be vigilant.

# If You have Questions:

Send your questions on North Carolina family law and divorce matters to **"Ask Carolyn ..."** at askcarolyn@rhinotimes.com, or P.O. Box 9023, Greensboro, NC 27427. Please do not put identifying information in your questions. Note that the answers in "Ask Carolyn" are intended to provide general legal information, and the answers are not specific legal advice for your situation.

A subtle fact in your unique case may determine the legal advice you need in your unique case. Also, please note that you are not creating an attorney-client relationship with Carolyn J. Woodruff by writing or having your question answered by **"Ask Carolyn ..."** "Ask Carolyn" will be a regular column, but not necessarily weekly, and may use hypothetical questions.

## The Seven Nights of Santa

**Authors**
Dwight A. Ensley and Carolyn J. Woodruff

*The Seven Nights of Santa* is a holiday book for small children, their parents, grandparents, and caregivers. Today's family units encompass a large variety of family forms. Many children do not live with both of their natural parents. This leads to much stress and dispute during the holidays, particularly as to which house Santa will deliver toys and other presents.

In *The Seven Nights of Santa*, Captain Green Eyes resolves the issue for his little Cupcake Buddies and for Cupcake Buddies everywhere. For 7 nights, Santa can come to different houses and deliver toys and other presents. With the Santa list for each home in hand, all a child must do is tell Santa what night to come to which home. Each parent, grandparent, or caregiver can share with the child the surprises left by Santa under the tree at that home.

The mission of Captain Green Eyes is to help all the little Cupcake Buddies out there to accept and love their family units regardless of form. We hope this book will bring to you and your Cupcake Buddies more happiness, kindness, understanding, and love.

## Ask Carolyn ... Straight Talk from the Dancing Divorce Attorney

### Author, Carolyn J. Woodruff

*Ask Carolyn ... Straight Talk from the Dancing Divorce Attorney* is a book of practical wit and wisdom for today's family challenges. The book contains mostly Ask Carolyn columns from the *Rhino Times* newspaper.

The book talks about varied family law matters. "She finally admitted having oral sex with the suspect ..." "Can I deduct the $2,500 as alimony on my income taxes?" "I have a very young child who has been the victim of sexual offenses." Carolyn Woodruff, a North Carolina Board Certified Family Law Specialist, CPA, and business valuator answers North Carolina family law questions in a candid, and often inspiring, way.